# THE MENTAL SHIFT

**Books by Darrin Donnelly**

*THINK LIKE A WARRIOR*

*OLD SCHOOL GRIT*

*RELENTLESS OPTIMISM*

*LIFE TO THE FULLEST*

*VICTORY FAVORS THE FEARLESS*

*THE TURNAROUND*

*THE MENTAL GAME*

*THINK BIG TO WIN BIG*

*THE MENTAL SHIFT*

# THE MENTAL SHIFT

CONTROL YOUR THOUGHTS,
CONTROL YOUR DESTINY

Darrin Donnelly

Copyright © 2026 by Darrin Donnelly.

All rights reserved.

Published in the United States by Shamrock New Media, Inc.

All rights reserved. No part of this publication may be reproduced in any form by any means, in whole or in part, without the prior written consent of Shamrock New Media, Inc. This includes reprints, excerpts, photocopying, recording, or any other means of reproducing text. If you would like to do any of the above, please seek permission by contacting us at: info@sportsforthesoul.com

Limit of Liability/Disclaimer of Warranty: This publication contains statements and statistics believed to be reliable, but neither the author(s) nor the publisher can guarantee the accuracy or completeness of any of the information contained in this publication. No warranty is made with respect to the accuracy or completeness of the information contained herein. The strategies outlined in this publication may not be suitable for every individual, and are not guaranteed or warranted to produce any particular results. The author(s) and publisher specifically disclaim any responsibility for any liability, loss, or risk, personal or otherwise, which is incurred as a consequence, directly or indirectly, of the use and application of any of the contents of this publication.

This book is a work of fiction. The names, characters, places, teams, organizations, and events are either products of the author's imagination or used fictitiously to enhance the setting.

Unless specifically stated elsewhere, this book is not officially associated with, endorsed by, affiliated with, or sponsored by any of the individuals, entities, companies, teams, or organizations written about in this book.

Sports for the Soul is a registered trademark of Shamrock New Media, Inc.

Cover design: Damonza
Cover images: Shutterstock

ISBN: 979-8-9880102-2-7

Library of Congress Control Number available upon request.

Visit us at: SportsForTheSoul.com

# Sports for the Soul®

This book is part of the *Sports for the Soul* series. For updates on this book, future books, and a free newsletter that delivers advice and inspiration from top coaches, athletes, and sports psychologists, join us at: **SportsForTheSoul.com**.

The *Sports for the Soul* newsletter will help you:

- Find your calling and follow your passion
- Harness the power of positive thinking
- Build your self-confidence
- Attack every day with joy and enthusiasm
- Develop mental toughness
- Increase your energy and stay motivated
- Explore the spiritual side of success
- Be a positive leader for your family and your team
- And much more…

Join us at: **SportsForTheSoul.com**.

*To Laura, Patrick, Katie, and Tommy;*

*who are everything to me.*

# Introduction

We've all been there.

You're cruising through life. You're feeling good, working hard, and staying positive. You're on a winning streak, hitting nothing but fairways and greens. It seems like everything is going your way. You've got it all figured out.

Then, you suddenly get blindsided by adversity.

You lose a key client. A health issue shows up out of nowhere. The marketing strategies you've used in the past abruptly stop working. Your company gets bought out and you lose your job through no fault of your own. Bad news about a loved one suddenly requires all of your attention. Accidents. Injuries. Uncontrollable changes.

Overnight, it seems like those fairways and greens you've been hitting have turned into bunkers and ponds.

Whatever the cause, that winning streak you've been on collapses into a losing streak, and now you feel lost. You can't figure out why this is happening or what you're doing wrong.

It happens to us all.

Life has an uncanny way of throwing adversity at us right when we think problems just might be a thing of the past.

When things go wrong, we often lose control of our thinking. Thoughts of worry, self-doubt, anger, and panic can take over our minds. We worry that this new problem may never go away, that all that was good may never come back. We question our decisions, our worthiness, and our abilities. We get angry about what we can't control. We enter a mental state of fear, stress, and panic.

Why is this happening? Was all our hard work a waste of time and effort? Was all our optimism nothing more than wishful thinking? What if our best days are behind us and never coming back?

These are the types of thoughts that make a tough situation tougher. They make us feel helpless, as though we no longer have any control over what might happen next.

Instead of going down such a negative path, there is one question above all others you should be asking yourself when life hits you with an obstacle you didn't see coming: **How can I get back on track and overcome this obstacle in the fastest way possible?**

This book will show you how to do exactly that.

I know that sounds like a big promise, but I spend my life researching the differences between those who rise to the top and those who fall by the wayside. In sports, business, and life, the most successful people I've studied and interviewed respond differently—*much* differently—than the not-so-successful when faced with adversity.

What separates them isn't luck or talent.

It's the way they *choose* to respond. It's the way they *choose* to think when faced with adversity.

**Top achievers haven't figured out a way to avoid more adversity than everyone else, they've figured out a way to bounce back *faster* and without losing their confidence or focus along the way.**

When you get blindsided by a negative event—whether it's suddenly losing your golf swing or something much more serious—you must remember that how you *respond* to the adverse event makes all the difference.

**Your life will follow your most dominant thoughts. But it's easy to forget that during times of stress and panic.**

To get back on track, the first thing you must do is take control of your thoughts and shift your mindset from a negative state of helplessness to a positive state of empowerment.

You must make a mental shift before you can attack your problem effectively. This book will reveal what that shift is and exactly how to do it.

**In the pages that follow, you will learn how to overcome setbacks quickly, confidently, and positively.**

With golf as the metaphor for life, *The Mental Shift* will walk you through a powerful process for attacking any adversity you face.

Told as a relatable fable, this book follows up with characters first featured in one of my previous books, *The Mental*

*Game*.

Just as pro golfer Jack McKee has become one of the top players on the PGA Tour, a freak car accident has left him with devastating injuries. Through no fault of his own, his world has been turned upside down and everything that was going so well for him has been taken away. His comeback attempt has been a disaster and Jack is now worried his career is over.

Questioning all the positive-thinking techniques he once embraced, Jack reconnects with his old mentor, the legendary golfer Eddie Collins, who teaches him a powerful method for shifting his mindset, taking back control of his future, and quickly overcoming life's setbacks.

**How should you respond when everything that had been going well suddenly turns on you?**

That is what this book answers.

If *The Mental Game* was the guide to developing a positive self-image and training your mind with powerful self-talk, *The Mental Shift* is the advanced course on how to respond when that new mindset gets put to the ultimate test.

Whatever adversity you may be dealing with right now—whether it's something as serious as a job loss or health crisis, or a classic case of the yips on the golf course—**this book will show you how to take back control of your life quickly and confidently**.

This isn't about pretending everything is fine.

It's about learning how to respond when it isn't.

In sports, in business, and in life, **you can't change what happened, but you *can* change what happens next!**

The power to take back control begins with a simple shift in your thinking. This book will show you how to do it.

Darrin Donnelly
*SportsForTheSoul.com*

*"The real test in life, as in golf, is not in keeping out of the rough but in getting out after we've hit one in the tall grass. Championships, in games and in life, are won by those who have learned to cope with adversity."*

- OG MANDINO

# 1

"I feel great," I muttered to myself through gritted teeth as I stomped my way up to the 18th green on this mid-May afternoon at the prestigious Quail Hollow Club in Charlotte, North Carolina.

"I feel *great,*" I forced myself to whisper again, spitting the words through pursed lips, still unable to believe the lie I was telling myself.

"What's that?" my caddie and brother, Mike, asked me from behind.

I shook my head and waved him off. "Nothing."

I had just chipped my way onto the green. My ball rolled to a stop nine feet from the cup. Normally, I'd be fairly happy walking onto the green with a roughly fifty-fifty shot of making my first putt.

The problem was, my first putt would be my fifth shot on this hole. The hole was a par-4, which meant pro-level golfers were *supposed* to get that little white ball into the cup within four shots or less. The best I could hope for was a bogey (one shot above par) on my final hole of Round Two at the PGA Championship.

I took a deep breath, trying to exhale my frustration.

*What difference does any of this make, anyway?* I thought to myself. *You've already missed the cut. Just get out of here and put this horrible day behind you.*

On the PGA Tour, only a certain number of golfers make the cut after the first two rounds and get to compete in the third and fourth rounds on Saturday and Sunday. The PGA Championship's cut line was the top seventy players (plus ties). The score required to make the cut was 2 strokes over par—a score I had no shot at achieving.

I thought about all those self-talk techniques legendary golfer Eddie Collins had taught me. Not only was Eddie my childhood hero, but he had become a great friend and mentor of mine three years ago. He showed me how to take control of my thoughts. He told me there was a constant battle between the positive and negative in one's mind, and the side that won that battle would determine the direction of your life. He taught me the importance of talking to myself instead of listening to myself—speaking positively to myself instead of listening to the negative thoughts that tried to dominate my mind.

That man turned my career around.

But at this moment, I was seeing red and not trusting any of those techniques.

*What would Eddie say right now?*

*Oh, right ... this next shot will be my best shot. Stop thinking about the past, focus only on this moment.*

But I couldn't do it. I couldn't shift to a positive mental

state. I was too angry and my mind kept latching on to the negative.

*This embarrassing, disastrous moment.*

*What a pitiful case I have become.*

I was fuming as I knelt down to read the green. I felt a sharp pain in my lower back, something I had been dealing with since the accident. A constant reminder of the day my life changed in an instant.

Mike took a crouched position behind me with his hands on his knees, reading the green as well.

"Drops slightly to the left," he said to me. "I'd aim right of the hole just a bit."

"If you say so."

I wasn't being sarcastic with my brother. I honestly didn't see what he was seeing. I was so angry, I just wanted off the course.

Since my comeback attempt began six weeks ago, I had struggled to read the greens like I used to. I just couldn't find that line. And even when I did, it didn't seem to matter. My feel was off. I would hit it too hard or too slow. I would watch my ball go to the right or the left of my target.

This was a huge problem because if I was going to have any shot at still competing on the PGA Tour, I knew I would need to be a master of the short game. I was never a particularly long driver to begin with, but since the accident, my distance had taken a significant beating. My average drive was twenty yards less than it had been before the accident.

My back lacked the fluidity it used to have. I didn't have the torque I needed for the monstrous drives most pros are known for.

Nothing in my game had been the same since I was run over by a car thirteen months ago.

I lined up my putt and aimed right of the cup, blindly trusting my brother's guidance. I took my shot and, just before contact with the ball, felt an annoying twitch that disrupted the rhythm of my swing.

I watched my ball head towards the cup with much less speed than I intended. It was as though my shoulders had involuntarily hit the brakes just before I made contact with the ball.

I watched my ball break to the left in front of the hole and roll downhill, finally coming to a stop six inches from the hole as the small crowd watching groaned in sympathy for me.

I left my next shot short and then tapped in for a *triple*-bogey, finally closing the curtain on another debacle at a Major tournament for Jack McKee.

The comeback story I and most of the golf world had been rooting for over the past six weeks was clearly not to be.

What had been taken away from me wasn't coming back. I didn't belong on courses like this one anymore.

Truth is, even before the accident, I had developed a reputation for struggling at Majors. These were the four most prestigious golf tournaments of each PGA season: the Masters, the PGA Championship, the U.S. Open, and the British Open. My performance at this year's PGA Championship took my struggles at Majors to a new low.

My triple-bogey on the 18th gave me a score of 85 for the round. That was 14 strokes over the par 71 for Quail Hollow. *Fourteen* strokes.

Now, every golfer has a bad round from time to time. Even us pros who do this for a living. Breaking 80 is embarrassing for a pro, but it happens. Sometimes it just isn't your day.

What made this day's performance so much worse was that my first round had not been much better, when I shot an 82.

For the tournament—and again, not just any tournament, this was the PGA Championship, one of only four Major events held each year on the PGA Tour—I had shot 25 strokes over par. I finished dead last.

Dead.

Last.

To make the cut for Round Three, I would have had to shoot no worse than 2 strokes over par. I missed the cut by 23 freaking strokes. That's how bad I played.

It was the single worst two-round score of my professional career.

If I played this way at a local tournament with amateur players nobody had heard of, I would have walked away in shame. But this was against the best players in the world in front of a national TV audience. This was a *Major* tournament, which is supposed to showcase only the very best golfers in the world.

And here I was, making a mockery of the sport.

I picked up my ball and gave Mike a forced smile and shrug while I listened to a smattering of pity claps from the handful of fans watching.

"I'm glad that's over with," I said quietly to my brother. As I briefly locked eyes with him, I saw the worried look on his face. He knew my game was long gone and might never be coming back.

"Just wasn't our day," Mike said. "You'll get it back. It's a process. We'll start off better next time."

I nodded, knowing my brother and caddie was saying the only thing he could.

What Mike didn't know was that I wasn't sure there would be a next time.

I was tired of putting myself through this.

# 2

Shortly after my humiliating performance at the PGA Championship, I entered the large white tent set up for the press, stood at the podium, and answered questions from reporters. For a guy who finished dead last in the tournament, the tent was packed with media looking for a compelling story. Many in the tent were no doubt wondering if I was about to announce my early retirement.

"There isn't much I can say after a performance like that," I said to the group. "I played horribly from start to finish. Never had a chance out there. I haven't found any rhythm since returning to the Tour. I'm disappointed and embarrassed by the way I played today. With that, I'm open to any questions."

"How are you feeling health-wise?" a reporter shouted. "Are the injuries from your accident preventing you from finding your rhythm out there?"

"That's a safe bet. I never played this poorly before the accident."

"Are you in pain on the course?" another shouted.

"I feel it at times in my leg, my hip, my back, but I didn't think it was bad enough to withdraw. Maybe I should have."

"Jack, are you going to play in next week's tournament?"

"I'm registered to play, but I'll take it day by day. If my back starts acting up, I might have to bow out."

Though my left leg and hip suffered the worst of the car accident, it was my back that had been giving me the most trouble since my return to the Tour.

"Do you think you rushed your comeback?" a reporter asked.

"The results don't lie, do they?"

"Are you considering taking a break from the Tour to regroup and revaluate?" she followed up.

I shrugged and let out a sigh of defeat. "I've got to do something. I'm not sure exactly what. My play has been embarrassing. Again, the results don't lie."

"Can you tell us where you are mentally right now?" another asked.

I took a moment to contemplate and then answered as honestly as I could.

"Not good," I said. "Not good at all."

This was a side of me the press wasn't used to seeing. Ever since my first PGA tournament victory three seasons ago, I was usually positive and lighthearted when I interreacted with the media and fans.

Things had changed.

I took a few more questions about the state of my game

and future plans before one reporter finally asked the question everyone was waiting for someone to ask.

"Jack, based on your performance since your return to the Tour six weeks ago, do you fear this might be the end of your professional career?"

No need to dance around the issue. I again answered as honestly as I could.

"Yes. Yes, I do."

# 3

Just before the accident, my career had caught fire.

After thirteen years of struggling to make it as a pro golfer, I picked up my first PGA Tour victory at the Gateway Championship. That was three seasons ago. A few weeks after that first PGA win, I finished ninth overall in the season-ending Tour Championship.

The next season, I won three more PGA tournaments, notched a few top-five finishes on top of my wins, and signed my first sponsorship deal. I didn't play great at any Majors, but I finished fifth at the Tour Championship for my second top-ten finish in a row at the season-ending playoffs.

I was playing the best golf of my career and suddenly becoming recognized as one of the top golfers in the world. My wife, Ashley, and I were excited about the future. Our family was growing (we had our fourth child), we built the home of our dreams, and it felt like we were achieving all the big goals we had once fantasized about. I was happier than I'd ever been before.

The following season (last year), I was off to another strong start, notching three top-five finishes in the early stretch of the season.

Then, a week before the Masters, it happened.

I needed to get in some cardio and decided to take advantage of the unseasonably warm weather by going for a run a few blocks from my home in the suburbs of Kansas City. I had headphones on, listening to one of my favorite books about the importance of positive thinking as I jogged on the sidewalk, which ran alongside a nearby road.

I waved to the occasional driver who acknowledged me with a friendly wave, fist-pump, or honk. A few fellow joggers yelled out, "Good luck at the Masters," as they passed me with smiles.

Life was good.

It was such a beautiful day—sunny, breezy, and warm. The type of April afternoon in the Midwest where you can't wait to roll down the windows and crank up some tunes for the first time since winter.

I felt like I was running faster than normal, feeling lighter, like the warmer weather had loosened any winter stiffness.

That's when I heard a loud honk to my left.

I turned towards the honk, instinctively throwing a wave at what I assumed was somebody who recognized me. Instead, I saw a red-faced driver in the far lane, his hand holding down the horn in anger. In an instant, the driver in the lane closest to me and driving in the same direction I was running, swerved abruptly away from the honking car, and rushed my direction with no signs of stopping.

It all happened so fast.

The driver's car banged over the curb and slammed into my left leg before I could react. I fell to the ground, heard a loud crack as his front tire rolled over my lower leg, and hit my head with a thud before blacking out.

I woke up in an ambulance.

My left leg was in excruciating pain as an EMT sitting above me placed her hand on my forehead, trying to keep me still on the bumpy ride. I looked down—confused, panicked—and saw another EMT holding my lower left leg in place, lots of blood on my pants and all over the blue latex gloves he was wearing. It's funny what you remember.

Turns out, the driver who hit me had been texting while driving. The speed limit was 35 in this residential area. He was exceeding that speed limit while sending a text and crossing the centerline towards another driver, who honked furiously. The texter looked up in shock, swerved right, but overcorrected. He bounced over the curb and ran straight into me.

What are the odds that a driver at that very instant would veer onto the sidewalk at the exact moment I was running along that same sidewalk?

Had he not been texting, this never would have happened. Had I not been running right where I was running at the precise second I was, he would have gotten a good scare, maybe banged up his car a bit and promised himself never to text and drive again, but nobody would have been injured and that would have been that.

Why was I there at that exact moment? Why was he driving the way he was at that exact moment? What were the odds of both happening at the exact same time?

If I had started my run just a second or two later than I did that afternoon, I would have watched the commotion unfold in front of me, come home with an exciting story to tell, and nobody would have been harmed.

But no, things had to happen just the way they did.

Those were the thoughts consuming me in the months that followed as I rehabbed my broken ankle, fractured femur, and sore back.

I was told numerous times how "lucky" I was that it hadn't been worse. How the curb had slowed down the driver's speed. How it was such a good thing I hit my head on the grass instead of the cement. How if I hadn't turned just when I did, the impact could have done irreversible damage to my back. How just an inch one way or the other could have resulted in far worse injuries or even death.

On and on went the list of reasons for how lucky I was *supposed* to feel because things could have been so much worse.

But I couldn't get over how *un*lucky I was to have been in the accident at all.

Initially, doctors told me they weren't sure if I'd ever again be able to play golf at a high level. I refused to believe it—and I had plenty of supporters who encouraged me not to.

Eddie Collins, my brother, my wife, numerous friends of mine on the Tour—they all encouraged me with stories of resilience.

During my months of recovery and intense rehab training, I can't tell you how many times I heard the famous story of Ben Hogan.

He was the legendary golfer who had been named the Golfer of the Year in 1948, just before a devastating car wreck in February of 1949 nearly killed him. Hogan spent two months in the hospital, underwent multiple surgeries, and it was believed by many he would never walk again, let alone play competitive golf again.

Incredibly, Hogan was back on the course in December, played on the PGA Tour in January of 1950, and won the U.S. Open in June of the same year. He would go on to win five more Majors, including three in 1953.

Hogan's story is considered one of the greatest comebacks in sports history. It was a huge inspiration to me as I trained for my own miraculous return to the Tour.

But six weeks ago, when I finally returned to competitive play a week before the Masters, reality set in.

I barely made it through the first two rounds at the Valero Texas Open. Soreness in my lower back gave me problems I wasn't prepared for and my left leg was throbbing after two days of competition. I missed the cut by 9 strokes.

The inspirational return I, the media, and fans all over the world were hoping to see was not to be.

I told myself not to panic. I reasoned that the Valero Texas Open was supposed to be a higher-stakes practice round for me, something to get me ready for my *real* return to glory at the Masters the following week.

But at the Masters, I had to withdraw midway through the second round. By the time I withdrew, my lower back was so tender, even the slightest twist sent sharp pain through me and made me feel like it might lock up at any moment.

I took the next two weeks off, sticking to practice rounds only.

I returned to the PGA Tour for the CJ Cup Byron Nelson the first weekend of May. I actually shot a strong opening round, but fell apart on Friday and failed to make the cut by 2 strokes. At least I was improving, I told myself.

The next week, I played in the Truist Championship, but embarrassed myself by missing the cut by 11 strokes. Once again, my back soreness worsened as the rounds went on.

And that brings us to the PGA Championship, where I redefined what *embarrassed myself* could look like, missing the cut by 23 strokes.

My visions of hoisting trophies and inspiring the world with a Ben-Hogan-type comeback for the ages had faded.

Truth be told, I'm not sure I ever believed it would

happen.

Though I felt competent during practice rounds, I didn't feel like anything close to my old self. I tried to convince myself competing in actual PGA Tour events might give me some spark of competitive magic that would carry my play to new heights.

Turns out, that was nothing more than wishful thinking.

Now, I was making a mockery of the sport, becoming a pitiful case of someone who didn't belong on the same course with the *real* Tour pros. I saw the sympathetic eyes as fellow players nodded at me in the locker room and on the course.

"What a sad case," they must have been thinking. "What a shame what happened to Jack McKee. Is anyone gonna tell this guy it's time to hang it up?"

My victories from two seasons ago had earned me a Tour Card exemption that would only last through the rest of the current season. After that, I'd have to earn my way back on to the Tour with fresh victories or strong finishes.

For a guy who had just played the worst two rounds of his professional career, it was time to acknowledge reality.

There wasn't going to be any miraculous comeback. I wasn't going to capture any inexplicable magic simply by walking onto a PGA Tour course and *believing* in myself.

My game was gone. My career was over. Almost as quickly as it had all come together for me three seasons ago, the universe came along and took it away from me.

It wasn't right.

I was bitter. I was angry.

I was tired of all the pain and humiliation.

The sport I had loved since I was a kid was now a cruel reminder of all that had unfairly been taken away from me.

I was in a miserable state, wishing I had never tasted success in the first place. Because then, I would have never really known what living my dream felt like.

The year-and-a-half prior to my accident was the best period of my life. I woke up most mornings feeling joy, excitement, and gratitude, knowing I was living the life I had always dreamed of. It was heaven on earth.

And now it was gone.

All of it was gone.

These days, I often woke up with an immediate sense of dread and despair, resentful of the fact the accident and everything since hadn't been a bad dream I was waking up from.

Golf was now my daily reminder of what I once had and would never have again.

It was time to walk away from the game I once loved.

# 4

"Did you talk to Eddie?" Mike said.

A couple hours after my pitiful performance at the PGA Championship, Mike and I were eating dinner at a Charlotte steakhouse miles from Oak Hollow Club. I didn't want to risk eating near the club and running into any other players or media members. I knew well-meaning people might try to lift me up with pep talks, but I didn't want to hear it.

"I got a text from him," I said. "You know Eddie, he told me the same old stuff: put the tournament behind me, focus on what's next, find the opportunity in the situation—that sort of thing."

Long retired and now in his seventies, Eddie Collins was one of golf's greatest all-time players. His prime on the PGA Tour was back in the '80s and '90s and he had a great stretch on the Champions Tour (what was then called the Senior PGA Tour) after he turned fifty. His name is mentioned regularly with other legends of the game like Ben Hogan, Arnold Palmer, Jack Nicklaus, and Tiger Woods.

Fans loved Eddie not only for his impressive wins, but also for his laid-back attitude on the course and personable style off of it. He was one of those guys who loved life, exuded enthusiasm, and never met a stranger. He was a role model and a hero to many, including me.

Three years ago, I became close friends with my childhood hero. At a time when my career had reached a low-point (I suffered an embarrassing panic attack at a PGA tournament after missing the cut for the sixteenth-straight time), Eddie took me under his wing and mentored me through my crisis. He taught me that golf, like life, was ultimately a mental game. He showed me how to win that mental game by taking control of my self-talk and defeating that negative voice that promotes fears, worries, and anxiety.

Eddie saved my career.

A few months after he began coaching me, I won my first ever PGA tournament and my hot streak as a pro began.

I give all the credit for my sudden turnaround to Eddie Collins and his mentorship. He changed the way I thought. He changed the way I saw myself and the world around me.

After my accident, Eddie was the first person outside of my family members to show up at the hospital. He visited me often during my rehab months to encourage and guide me. He called or texted nearly every day as I began training again. He was always trying to brighten my mood and keep me from going down a dark path.

Some days, especially early on in the process, I

appreciated hearing from Eddie. His enthusiasm was contagious and his encouragement gave me hope. As time went on, however, there were more days when—and I hate to admit this—I wanted him to leave me alone. He was worried about me and convinced that keeping my mind in shape—positive, focused, and free of fear—was the most important component of my comeback.

But as my rehabilitation dragged on and I grew more frustrated with my situation, I stopped wanting to hear that.

I was grieving the career that had unfairly been taken away from me. Why had this happened to me? Why was I having to go through this grueling rehab for something that was in no way my fault?

At times I felt depressed and, frankly, all I wanted to do was complain and wallow in self-pity.

I know that sounds pathetic, but it's the truth.

If I'm being completely honest, I have to say there was a part of me that began to resent Eddie. Not because I didn't like, admire, and appreciate all he had done for me, but because I felt deceived by some of the things he had taught me.

He told me life would follow my thoughts and expectations. Well, I never *expected* to have some idiot crash his car into me as I went on a casual run.

He told me life tends to give back what we give it. Well, what had I done to deserve this accident?

He told me to trust that whatever happens *to* me was actually happening *for* me, that there is a greater opportunity to be found within every obstacle. Well, I didn't see how a freak car crash that ruined my career was providing me with any profound opportunities.

He told me positive thoughts led to positive results. Well, before the accident I had been staying plenty positive, but there was nothing positive about being run over by a careless driver.

I was questioning everything Eddie had taught me over the years.

His advice had worked for me before. It had given me a brighter outlook and a renewed hope about what my career could look like. But this brutal accident had changed everything.

In the months following the accident, there were days when I wondered why I should waste my time and energy trying to be positive and hopeful when something like this could come out of nowhere and take away everything I had worked so hard for. After frustrating training sessions or practice rounds, I questioned whether I was only making things worse by trying to force "toxic positivity" into my head when my life seemed to only be getting worse.

As the months of rehab and training went on, I distanced myself more and more from Eddie. I didn't ice him out. I was cordial and appreciative when I did talk to him, but I was growing colder toward him, shorter with my responses, deflective whenever he wanted to talk about my mental state.

He took the hint.

His calls became less and less frequent and now we only corresponded through occasional text messages. He would send me some type of encouraging message and I would respond with short, noncommittal replies.

Over the past six weeks, as I returned to the Tour, I tried to force myself to use the positive self-talk and the visualization techniques Eddie had taught me. But it all rang hollow in my mind. I no longer believed they could help me.

As I failed to see my results improve the way I wanted, I became convinced the mental techniques Eddie taught me were at best a waste of time and at worst only adding to my frustrated, stressed, and anxious mental state.

After every bad shot, I'd say to myself something along the lines of, *A lot of good my positive talk is doing,* and only get angrier that I couldn't control my situation better.

The pattern was driving me nuts and I feared where it was headed.

Stress, anxiety, and anger were consuming me. I sometimes found it hard to take a deep breath, not only on the course but even throughout the day when I wasn't playing. It was like a weight was crushing down on my chest.

I worried I was losing my livelihood. The career I had dreamed of having since I was a kid was being taken away from me just when I had finally reached it. *What would I do next with my life?*

I feared I had overextended myself financially, now wondering if our family would have to move out of the dream house we had built when things were going well. *Was I being punished for dreaming too big and chasing the life I had dreamed of?*

Sometimes at night, lying in bed, I'd suddenly get overwhelmed with a jolt of worry about the future or anger about what had happened. My entire body would tense up, my stomach would drop, and I would feel as though a furnace had been turned on inside me. Sweat would form on my forehead and tears would well up in my eyes. *I can't believe this has happened to me,* my mind would repeat over and over.

This was no way to live. I was driving myself crazy. I was tired of thinking about my career and questioning why everything had gone so badly so quickly.

Three years ago, just before Eddie Collins began mentoring me, I suffered a very public panic attack and collapsed on the 18th green at the Charles Schwab Challenge. The same feelings that preceded that horrible moment were now boiling up again.

I worried I was getting dangerously close to having another panic attack, and I didn't want to go through that nightmare again.

# 5

"I don't hear you talk as much about Eddie lately," Mike said as he cut into his steak. "Everything okay there?"

"We don't talk like we used to," I said. "Mostly quick texts here and there. With everything I've been going through, I haven't had the time to visit with him much."

"Does he still help you with your mental game?"

I nodded and waved off Mike's concerns as I chewed on my steak. "Sure, sure. That's all he talks about. He believes it."

"What about you? Do you still believe it?"

I shrugged. "To a point. His advice saved my career. You know that better than just about anyone. But I think we can all agree my current struggles have a lot more to do with being hit by a car than whether I'm thinking enough positive thoughts."

"Still, you've been working so hard on getting physically back into the game, it can't hurt to work on the mental side as well, right?"

I knifed into my steak more aggressively than normal. "What do you want me to say? I tried. I really did. But it's hard to stay calm and positive when your game has gone to crap. You saw me these past two days. I don't belong out there. I'm a joke."

I was raising my voice and my knuckles turned white as I gripped my knife and fork unnecessarily tight. "Am I frustrated, angry, embarrassed? Yes! I can't play the way I used to and I can't do anything about it. No amount of wishful thinking is going to change that."

I banged my fist on the table and dropped my knife and fork onto my plate with a loud clank. I noticed heads turning our way at nearby tables.

"Take it easy, Jack," Mike said in a quiet voice as he motioned with his hands for me to tamp down my volume. "It's going to get better. It just takes time."

I exhaled and took a large drink of water, trying to calm myself down.

"I don't have time," I said. "Do I need to remind you my Tour card runs out at the end of this season? The way I'm playing, there's no way I can earn the points to keep my card for next year. What then? Go back to Q-school? Hope for another season on the Korn Ferry Tour? I don't belong there any more than I do here. I'm thirty-seven, not twenty-seven. I'm not going back to the mini-tours. I'm done grinding. I'm done with the whole damn thing."

"What are you saying?"

"I'm saying, we gave this comeback a shot. It didn't work out. Now I'm only embarrassing myself. I'm done."

"That's crazy talk."

"Crazy is what I'm going to be if I keep trying to force something that isn't working. You don't understand what I've been going through this past year. I had something so special going for me, and then poof—in an instant it was gone. Just like that. Almost like God himself came along and said, 'You had your run, now it's someone else's turn.'"

My brother leaned back in his chair, shaking his head. "Jack, it's only been six weeks."

"And I'm only getting worse. What I had is *never* coming back. I can feel it. It's gone. Long gone."

Mike's dejected face reminded me that his livelihood as a pro caddie also depended on me playing. If I lost, so did he. If I failed to earn, so did he. If I quit, so did he.

"I'm sorry," I said. "I know I strung you along this past year when you could've started caddying for someone else."

"That never even crossed my mind," he said.

I gave my brother a nod of genuine appreciation. "I'm sorry to let you down, Mike. I just can't do this anymore. The pressure. The pain. The humiliation." I clinched my fist again. "I'm tired of caring so much. I'm tired of trying so hard. I'm tired of being angry at the guy that ran into me, angry at myself, angry at God. I'm tired of hoping and praying that today will be the day I get back on track. I get a glimmer of hope here and there, and then I fall apart again. I can't take it anymore."

"You're angry because of the way you played today.

You need to give it some more time."

I shook my head. "Truth is, I knew as soon as I walked on the course six weeks ago this wasn't going to work. I was praying for a miracle. I thought maybe stepping on a course in tournament play would give me some competitive jolt and I'd find my way back. Didn't happen. Things only got worse. It's time for me to hang it up."

Neither of us spoke for a moment. I think Mike had suspected this decision might be coming. He too had been desperately hoping for a miracle.

"What does Eddie think of this new plan of yours?" Mike asked.

"I haven't told him."

"Don't you think you owe it to him?"

I nodded. "I'm heading there tomorrow."

# 6

On a day when I should have been playing in the third round of the PGA Championship with about seventy of my fellow professional golfers, I flew to Austin, Texas, to visit Eddie Collins at his home—a beautiful Mediterranean-style estate that backed up to the PGA-level golf course he helped design. I had dinner with Eddie and his wife, Debbie. We caught up on how both of our families were doing. Eddie and I then went out to his patio to discuss what I had come to discuss.

Debbie left us to talk alone. She knew how badly I had been struggling on the course and wasn't surprised by my short-notice visit. She knew I needed a chat with her husband, my old mental coach.

"I suppose I should ask what brings you out here, but I probably don't need to," Eddie said.

Though I had not visited Eddie's place since the accident, in the past when I came for advice our routine was always the same. We'd catch up over dinner, then head out back where we'd sit by his pool, high atop a hill that overlooked a running creek and the 16th green of the course he designed. We'd have cold drinks as the sun went down and the stars came out.

Though in his mid-seventies, Eddie still moved with purpose and looked at least fifteen years younger than he was. He still exuded that youthful enthusiasm he'd always been known for. He loved to laugh and reminisce while sharing old stories. It felt good to be around him. In the past when I visited Eddie, I came away feeling happier and calmer, like I could see life clearer.

I wasn't so sure I'd feel that way after this visit.

"Actually, you might be surprised why I'm here," I said.

Eddie opened his hand towards me, giving me a the-floor-is-yours gesture.

I took a deep breath. "This isn't easy. I'm just gonna come right out and say it. I've decided to retire."

Eddie tilted his head back, trying to get a read on me. Then he smiled big.

"Golfers don't retire, Jack. We get told we're no longer welcome to play. Then, we join the Champions Tour. And when that's done, we just keep on playing whatever course we're allowed onto until one day somebody comes out and wheels our old, tired bodies off the course because we can no longer do it ourselves."

"As nice as that sounds, it's not true for everybody. I'm done. I tried to come back from the accident, but I'm only embarrassing myself out there. I can't take it anymore."

Seeing how serious I was, Eddie's smile faded from his face—a deeply tanned face that was apparently still spending plenty of time in the bright Texas sun as he continued to play the game he loved.

"Jack, you had a rough outing this week. It happens to everyone. You're only six weeks into your comeback. It takes time."

"Yeah, yeah, I know all that. This is different. I can feel it. What I once had is gone. The accident took something away and it's not coming back. My career is over. Fighting that reality is only making me crazy. I'm getting angrier and angrier about what happened to me and how helpless I feel not being able to do anything about it. When I step onto the course, it's an instant reminder of what I lost, what I can no longer do. I'm full of rage inside. If I don't quit now, I'm going to destroy myself from the inside out."

"I had a feeling you weren't being completely honest with me these last few months, but I had no idea you were this ... *angry* inside."

"I know I've been standoffish with you. It's not because I don't appreciate all your help; I do. It's just that, what I'm dealing with now isn't mental, it's all physical. The accident changed me and no amount of optimism or positive self-talk is going to fix this problem. Frankly, I'm starting to resent anyone who suggests that it could."

"I suppose I'm one of those people," Eddie said with an almost-apologetic smile. "I believe the physical and the mental are interconnected, always have been and always will be."

"I know you do, Eddie. And I've heard the same from my doctors, the two swing coaches I worked with, my personal trainer, another mental coach I was referred to—no offense."

Eddie chuckled. "None taken."

"They all say the same stuff, but I just don't buy it anymore. Not in this case. There are limits to what our beliefs and mindset can help us do."

Eddie gave me a grin. "For the record, you've just stated a very limiting belief."

I fought the urge to roll my eyes. I didn't want to hear this stuff. I gave a sigh and an indifferent shrug.

"Everyone has their opinions," I said. "All I know is I've tried everything. No matter how many hours I spend practicing, how positive I try to be, how many prayers I say, or how many changes I try to make to my swing, *nothing* is helping. And when I start each day and see that nothing is changing, it only makes me angrier. I feel like I'm about to explode.

"I can't take the stress anymore. It's going to ruin what's left of my health. I have to face reality and walk away. Find something else to do with my life. The universe threw me a bad break. It's not fair, but it happens. It is what it is."

Eddie leaned back and looked me in the eye, like he was sizing me up.

"Jack, I don't think you came all this way to tell me you're retiring."

"No?" I forced a chuckle. "And why is it you think I'm here?"

"I think there's something inside you that wants ... help. I think deep down you want me to tell you what you knew I would tell you."

"And what is that?"

"That it's too early to retire, that now is the time to stand up and *fight,* and that I can help you get back on track."

When Eddie said the words *stand up and fight,* chills went up my spine and into my shoulders. My eyes nearly welled up with tears. Something about those words broke through the bitterness I was feeling inside. At least for a brief moment. Something about my old friend's words gave me just a little hope—hope that I *desperately* needed.

"Am I right?" Eddie said.

"You know more about the subconscious than anyone I know," I said. "I came here to tell you I'm retiring; felt I owed it to you to tell you face-to-face. But if you've got some magical strategy you think can help me, I am all ears."

"There's nothing magical about it. But the way it works might feel like magic."

I felt the wound-up tension in my chest release—physical tension I had been walking around with for who knows how long. It was as though I could take a full deep breath for the first time in weeks.

Could my old mentor really have the solution to my problems?

The idea that there was *something* I might be able to do to change my situation gave me a boost of excitement. I suddenly had hope that the great Eddie Collins was about to reveal a secret that could maybe—*just maybe*—help me turn things around.

# 7

Almost as quickly as that jolt of hope lifted me up, the skeptical voice inside me spoke out.

"Eddie, if you had a strategy that could help me turn things around, why didn't you tell me this before?"

"Every time I tried I got the distinct sense you didn't want to hear it," Eddie said. "Was I wrong?"

I lowered my eyes, realizing now I had not done a very good job of hiding my resistance to Eddie's offers to help me over the past several months.

"No, you weren't wrong," I said. "I've been in a dark place. Bitter about what happened. I still am.

"I'm afraid to get my hopes up. This past year, every time I've allowed myself to feel hopeful about something, I end up seeing those hopes crushed. Each time it happens I get angrier. I'm tired of going through the ups and downs.

"That's why, even now, I'm not sure I want to hear about this strategy of yours. If I get my hopes up again and it doesn't work, I'm afraid I'm going to lose it."

"The only thing I can promise you is that I've seen this strategy work time and time again whenever life has dealt me or my loved ones a crisis—one of those obstacles that comes out of nowhere and really rattles you, makes you question everything you thought you knew.

"But you've got to be open to it. No amount of advice is going to help someone who refuses to accept it. You have to trust me, and you have to go all in. You've got to be willing to implement the entire strategy, not just certain parts of it."

"I'm intrigued, Eddie. Maybe that's just my desperation talking, but I'm very intrigued.

"It's not enough to be intrigued. I need you to trust me, and I need you to go *all in* with each step of this process. Otherwise, it's not going to work for you and I'll only be wasting your time and mine."

Eddie's stern eyes portrayed certainty. Whatever this strategy was, he was convinced it worked.

"You saved my career before," I said. "I'd be a fool not to trust you again."

Eddie extended his hand.

I shook it.

"Let's get started," he said.

# 8

Eddie leaned forward, his elbows on the table between us. The sun had fallen, the stars were out, and the ambient blue glow of Eddie's lit-up swimming pool reflected off his excited face. He could barely contain his enthusiasm.

"This is going to be fun," he said. "And I think you could use a little fun in your life right now."

I chuckled. "Yes, I suppose I could."

"Let me tell you a little story," Eddie said. "Back in the nineties—1996, to be exact—I was going through a very tough time. Ninety-five had been a great year for me. I was the top earner on the Tour. I won two Majors. I was in a perfect rhythm on the course. When the season ended, I couldn't wait to get started again. But I'd also been dealing with some lower back pain. A doctor convinced me to get what he called a 'very minor' surgery that would fix me right up. I would take a couple months off in the offseason and be back better than ever. That was the plan.

"When I returned to play in '96, everything that had been working stopped working. My swing was off, my back was worse than *before* the surgery, and for some damn reason I couldn't read the greens anymore. I was out of rhythm and mad at myself for having an optional surgery that only made things worse. I had been playing great despite my back soreness the year before, why didn't I leave well enough alone? I started doubting myself. I'm shanking balls all over the place. If there was a bunker on the course, my ball would find it. One of those stretches."

"I'm familiar with those," I said.

Eddie laughed. I did not.

"I missed six of the first eight cuts that season," Eddie said. "And it didn't get better as the spring went on. I finished something like fiftieth at The Players Championship and didn't make the cut at the Masters in April. Here I was, the number-one ranked golfer in the world heading into the season, my smiling face on all the commercials, fans paying their hard-earned money to see me play, and I was missing the cut and leaving before the weekend rounds even began. I was embarrassed. I was frustrated. I was disappointed in myself for letting down all the fans who had been so good to me.

"The pain in my back was worse, not better, and no matter how much time I spent practicing I couldn't get the feel for my swing back. I was forty-six at the time and starting to wonder if my time on the PGA Tour was over. I was mad at myself, mad at the doctor who operated on me, mad that all the success I was having seemed to be taken from me overnight. I wasn't ready for it to be over, so I got all angry and bitter about my situation, just like you. I thought long and hard about leaving the Tour.

"That's when my old man gave me some advice I'll never forget.

"After the Byron Nelson tournament up in Dallas, he and I had dinner. I told him about all my problems, how I had lost whatever I once had, how I wasn't sure I would even finish this season, how I might just wait for the Senior Tour in a few years. Any of this sound familiar?"

I nodded.

"Now, my dad was one of those old-school tough guys," Eddie said. "He grew up dirt-poor during the Depression. His family had no indoor plumbing, very little education, all that. He worked in the oil fields all his adult life. Hard, hard work in the Texas heat.

"He was also one of those guys who never complained. Always looked on the bright side of things. *Loved* his weekend golf games at the local municipal.

"My point is, a guy who grows up like my old man doesn't have a whole lot of sympathy for whining, especially when it's coming from a guy who has made his living playing a game. And let me tell you, all I was doing during our dinner was whining about this and that, feeling sorry for myself and complaining about everything that was going wrong for me."

Eddie paused for a moment and raised his eyebrows towards me, as if to ask if that too sounded familiar.

He continued. "So, as I finish telling him about all my

woes, he looks at me and says something I'll never forget."

I leaned in, anxious to hear the life-changing advice his father had given him.

"He tells me, 'Son, life isn't fair. Things are going to happen to you that you don't deserve. But just remember this. **You don't have the power to change anything that happened in the past, but you always have the power to change what happens *next*. Stop complaining. Go out there and change what happens next.**'

"When he said that, something shifted inside me. It was like an instant mental shift from feeling helpless to feeling powerful. I realized there are a lot of things I can't change, but there are plenty of things I can. I do have the power to change my life. I'm not a helpless victim. I went from feeling like I had no control over my future to the empowering feeling that I do.

"I realized that for the past six months my dominant thoughts had been on all the things I had no control over. Negative things that had happened in the past, which could not be changed, and helpless feelings about the future, acting as if my future had already been determined and I had no control over it.

"In an instant, when my old man reminded me that I had no power to change what happened in the past, but I *did* have the power to change what happened next, I started thinking about everything I might be able to change from here on out.

"When you're looking forward, when you're thinking about the infinite possibilities of the future, you have a choice you can make. **You can focus on what you *want* to happen in the future or on what you *don't* want to happen. The future you focus on the most will determine the trajectory of your life.**

"That's where power lies, Jack. Regardless of what has happened in the past, you *always* have the power to change what happens next."

Eddie leaned back and let me soak in what he was saying. I took a deep breath. The clear Texas night air was finally cooling off as the sky grew darker and the stars brighter. The smells of something delicious cooking at a nearby restaurant—probably the clubhouse where Eddie and I had shared many meals in the past—wafted around us.

"So, what *did* happen next?" I asked.

"To me, on the Tour? I got my act together. I did a lot of research on the mind-body connection for my back. I did a lot of reevaluating and realized how negative my mindset had become, how much I was looking backward instead of forward, how much I was looking to blame others for my past instead of taking responsibility for what I could do about my future. Over the next several months, I completely shifted my mindset from dark to light, from helpless to hopeful, from negative to positive.

"By the end of the season, my back was better, my swing

was back on track, and my short game was on target. I won two tournaments down the final stretch and ended up winning the Tour Championship to close the season. That may have been the single most satisfying victory of my life because it proved to me once again just how powerful this mental stuff really is.

"This stuff works, Jack. **Your life moves in the direction of your most dominant thoughts. If you want to change your life, you have to make a mental shift and change what you're thinking about most.**

"I've watched you play this season. You still have all the physical capabilities you need. Hell, you're still driving the ball farther than I ever did. The only thing holding you back is you. I believe if you shift your thinking, you can become an even *better* player than you were before.

"You have the power to do this. But first you have to shift your mindset. You have to change your thinking if you want to change your life.

"Keep your focus on the past and everything that has gone wrong, and you give up your power. Shift your focus to the future and everything you want to see happen, and you reclaim your power.

"Now let me ask you, Jack, where has your dominant focus been lately?"

# 9

I took a moment to consider Eddie's question. I had learned over the last few years that if I wanted to benefit from Eddie's help, I needed to be as honest as possible. It did me no good to hide my true thoughts.

"I admit, I've been more focused on the past," I said. "How can I not be after what happened? I'm constantly saying to myself, 'I can't *believe* this has happened. *Why* did this happen? *What* did I do to deserve this?' That sort of thing. I know it isn't healthy.

"But let me ask you something, Eddie. You just told me life will follow my dominant thoughts. Ever since I've known you, you've been telling me, 'What you focus on most tends to come about.' I've believed you. But then this horrible accident happened. Doesn't that prove your theory wrong? I was never walking around thinking, 'Hmm, I wonder if some idiot driver is going to crash into me today, shatter my leg, mess up my back, and ruin my career?' If life follows my dominant thoughts, where the hell did this accident come from?"

Eddie responded without missing a beat, ready to answer a question he had clearly pondered plenty during his lifetime.

"I'm sure there are some mental coaches or self-help gurus out there who would claim you were subconsciously fearing something bad might come along and ruin your career. Perhaps fearing that things were going so well you were now due for a setback. 'What you fear is what you create,' they will say.

"Personally, I don't think this mental stuff is *that* precise. Our mind may be our most powerful weapon, but I don't think the cause-and-effect of our thinking works quite like that. I'm not saying I know for sure, but that's my belief based on my experiences. We all constantly have fears floating in and out of our minds. It's part of being human. It would be chaos if our fears were always coming to fruition.

"I also don't believe God looked at Jack McKee and said, 'You know what? That guy is enjoying life a little too much right now, let me send a car accident his way and watch how he deals with it.'

"Again, I might be wrong. I'm not a theologian. I don't have all the spiritual answers. But I personally don't buy a concept like that. There are a lot of mysteries I don't think we'll ever know on this side of eternity and why God lets random bad things happen to good people is one of them.

"What I do believe is that fluke occurrences, freak accidents, and unfair events are always going to be part of life. There's nothing we can do to completely avoid all problems, challenges, and obstacles. Frankly, life would be pretty boring if we could.

"The point to remember is there are going to be lots of things that happen that you have no control over. It's the price of doing business in this world. The sooner you accept this, the better off you'll be.

"You're only going to end up angry and bitter if you go through life expecting positivity—or anything else—to prevent any and all adversity from occurring. Life doesn't work like that.

"You can be the most positive, most talented, most faith-filled, hardest-working person on the planet and you're still going to have adversity show up when you least expect it. That's simply a part of life, something we can't control no matter how hard we try.

"But—and this is the important part—I believe that **what happens to us is much less important than how we *respond* to what happens to us**. That's why I've always told you to expect problems, but expect to overcome them.

"You overcome problems by first shifting your focus from the problem to the solution. From what has gone wrong to what you can make right. From where you are to where you want to be.

"That's how you take back control of your life.

"The faster you can make this mental shift, the faster you'll overcome whatever adversity you're facing.

"Jack, your life *will* move in the direction of your most dominant thoughts. But this doesn't mean you can control every single thing that happens to you. You can get in your car right now and set your GPS for Dallas. Following those directions, you'll eventually hit Dallas. That doesn't mean you are guaranteed to avoid all obstacles along the way. Through no fault of your own, you might run into traffic slowdowns, get a flat tire, or even have to take some detours here and there, but as long as you keep following that GPS, you will eventually hit Dallas.

"That's how our dominant thoughts work. They set the GPS for the destination you want to reach in life. **There will be road blocks and obstacles, sometimes even freak accidents, but as long as you stay focused on where you *want* to end up and adjust your route as needed, your life will keep moving in the direction you are most focused on.** If you're focused on the road blocks, the obstacles, the accidents, and everything that is behind you, *that's* where you'll end up.

"No matter what comes your way, stay focused on where you want to end up and you'll eventually get there. I really believe that.

"**Obstacles will still come between you and your destination, but it's how you *respond* to them that determines where you end up.**

"Life will follow your most dominant thoughts. When you understand that, you'll understand the importance of shifting your thinking away from the anger, the negative, and all the things you *don't* want to happen."

# 10

It was easy for me to see that my dominant thoughts since the accident had been on all the things that had gone wrong. Sure, I had moments of fantasizing about how I might be able to make a comeback that would inspire the sports world, but my *dominant* thoughts were on all the problems I was dealing with. My *dominant* emotion was anger for having been put in a situation where such problems even existed.

Of course, recognizing this and being able to do something about it were two different things.

"What you're saying makes sense," I said. "And I admit, I've been in a dark place, focusing on the wrong things. But again, how can I not be? How can I not be upset that life dealt me such a bad hand out of nowhere? How can I not be ticked off every morning when I wake up to a level of soreness I didn't have before the accident? How can I not worry about my results when I keep playing so poorly? How do I focus on what I *want* to happen when so much bad *is* happening?"

"Here is the first step you must take," Eddie said. **"When life hits you with extreme adversity—especially**

**adversity you didn't see coming—the first thing you need to do is be kind to yourself."**

"Be kind to myself?" I slumped back in my chair, my enthusiasm deflating. This was not the earth-shattering secret to success I was hoping to hear. "That's it? That's your big advice for bouncing back?"

Eddie laughed. "It's the first step. I know it sounds simple, but it's the *crucial* first step. The longer you wallow in anger, self-pity, and bitterness, the longer you will delay your comeback.

"Your biggest problem right now is all the anger you are carrying. You're angry at the guy who hit you. You're angry your past beliefs didn't protect you from this crisis. You're angry at the horrible luck life dealt you.

"Anger is a perfectly reasonable initial reaction to adversity. In the short-term it can even give you an adrenaline boost that helps you overcome an obstacle. But after a while anger isn't going to do you any good. When you allow it to consume you, it only makes life harder. It creates a prison for yourself, trapping you from making your situation better.

"Whether you get betrayed by someone you trusted, cheated by someone you didn't, hit by an incompetent driver, or simply blindsided by random bad luck, holding on to anger—no matter how validated your anger might be—eventually isn't going to hurt anyone other than you.

"The anger you feel inside is preventing you from

getting on with your life and attacking your problem in the most efficient way possible. It's keeping you focused on the past and not the future. It's keeping you focused on the problem and not the solution.

"You have to stop beating yourself up and start being kind to yourself. You didn't do *anything* wrong to cause the problem you're dealing with. Like a sudden gust of wind that blows your perfect shot into the lake, there was nothing you did to cause this to happen. And that's the worst kind of adversity—when it's something that happened through no fault of your own. Unfortunately, such things happen.

"But holding on to anger or wallowing in self-pity is just a way to keep hurting yourself for something that wasn't your fault. You were not responsible for what happened. **What you *are* responsible for is what happens next.** That's where your power is. In the present."

I took a moment to consider what Eddie was saying.

"But how can I not feel this way when I think about how unlucky I was?" I said. "I was doing everything right. I was working hard, being disciplined, staying positive, focusing on the future I wanted, trusting God, all those things. And yet, this freak accident came along and took away everything I had worked so hard for."

"The answer to your question was in your question."

I gave Eddie a blank look.

He smiled. "You just asked, 'How can I not feel this way when I *think* about how unlucky I was?' Well, you *will* feel angry when you choose to think about how unlucky you were. The answer is to stop thinking about it."

"Easier said than done," I said.

"Isn't everything worthwhile?"

"Fair point."

"It isn't easy, but you have to make that mental shift if you want to move from where you are to where you want to be.

"Thoughts of anger, questions about why this happened to you, the urge to keep blaming someone or something for what happened—these thoughts are going to keep coming up. The key is to remind yourself how harmful they are as soon as they do. Remind yourself that nothing good is going to come from ruminating on toxic thoughts like these. Remind yourself that every moment you think such thoughts is a moment holding you back from where you want to go.

"Don't grab on to them. Don't befriend them. Don't let them sit at the forefront of your mind.

"Right now, those thoughts are a coping mechanism. It can feel oddly empowering to blame or to be sad or to rage against the injustice of the situation. After all, you deserve to be mad about what happened. But you must remind yourself immediately that these thoughts are not your friends. They are *preventing* you from getting to where you want to be. They will ultimately reinforce a feeling of helplessness, which is one of the most destructive emotions you can ever have.

"**Emotions like anger, bitterness, self-pity, worry, fear that things will never get better—these are all negative emotions that keep you stuck.** It's kind of like driving your car with the parking brake on. You might make some progress, but it's going to be a lot slower and it's going to damage your car as you fight against the brake's tension. You have to release the brake before you can move forward quickly and smoothly.

"Here's how you release the brake. **As soon as you notice negative thoughts or feel the emotions they create, immediately remember the harm they are causing you. Then, picture them as images or words, take a deep breath, and imagine them dissipating right before your eyes. Or, you might want to envision them harmlessly floating by, right out of your mind as you breathe easy. Allow yourself to smile at them. They are just thoughts; you don't have to give them the attention they seek.**

"As you do this, you will start to lighten up. You will feel the brake release as you let go of the burden of these negative emotions.

"Try it, right now. Close your eyes. Breathe deep. And let them go. Imagine these thoughts dissipating into thin air or floating away without harming you any longer."

I chuckled awkwardly. "This feels a little weird for me to do in front of you."

"So be it. I'd rather you feel self-conscious than keep

feeling all that anger you're carrying around.

"Forget I'm even here. Just close your eyes. Breathe in the night air. Picture your anger dissipating."

I saw Eddie close his eyes as he lifted his face to the night sky and took a deep breath. I followed suit.

I took a few deep breaths in and out. As soon as I stopped thinking about how silly I felt, the familiar emotions about what had happened came roaring back into my mind.

My stomach dropped as I thought about my embarrassing scorecard from the day before. I fought the urge to cry as the feeling of being abandoned by God rose to the front of my mind. Then came that familiar anger at the driver who ran into me, at the hand life had dealt me. *Why did this have to happen?*

I caught myself, recognizing where my thinking was headed. My breath had turned shallow. My chest had tightened. My muscles had tensed.

This was exactly what Eddie was talking about.

I reminded myself to take a deep breath and, in my mind, I saw an image of the word ANGER in big red letters. I watched the letters slowly dissipate in front of me, dissolving into the air until I didn't see them any longer.

I felt ... better, lighter.

Then I saw a mental picture of my scorecard from the day before. I felt humiliation. I took another deep breath and imagined the score card blowing away in the wind until I couldn't see it all, just another harmless piece of paper floating away.

Again, I felt … better.

I took several more deep breaths, exhaling slowly as a word, image, or emotion dissipated or floated away.

Finally, I actually laughed out loud.

"Wow," I said as I opened my eyes. "This really works."

Eddie opened his eyes and smiled. "We're just getting started, my friend."

# 11

Eddie went inside to refill our drinks. It was turning into a beautiful summerlike night in Texas Hill Country.

When he left, I repeated the breathing and visualization technique he had just taught me. I actually smiled as certain negative images—images of the accident, images of a shanked shot, images of spectators shaking their heads in disappointment after one of my poor shots—floated away or dissolved. I smiled because as these images left my mind, I realized they were losing their power over me.

I didn't *have* to focus on them. I didn't *have* to dwell on them whenever they forced their way into my mind. I could simply ... let them go and watch them fade away as I exhaled.

It felt good.

Really good.

The more I did this visualization exercise, the more I noticed that, for the first time in months, the images were no longer giving me a surge of anger, bitterness, sadness, worry, or self-pity. They were just images, like old pictures I could turn the page on or throw away completely.

I was laughing to myself when I heard Eddie open the

door to the back patio. I opened my eyes.

"I can't believe how well this works," I said.

Eddie placed my drink in front of me and took a seat at the table. "It's amazing, isn't it? How such a simple technique can change your mental state so quickly? There will be times when it's not quite so effective, of course. The newness of the technique makes it particularly powerful right now, but as you know from the work you've done on your mental game in the past, those negative thoughts will keep coming back. Just make a point to recognize them and let them go as soon as they do. Once you do that, you can start replacing them with positive thoughts.

"When bad things occur, we all have a tendency to punish ourselves, even if we know whatever happened wasn't really our fault. We beat ourselves up for being at the wrong place at the wrong time or for not somehow seeing the trouble coming. Even if the problem *was* completely our fault, we replay our mistakes over and over again, reliving the pain, the humiliation, the guilt, and the grief.

"**One of the worst things we can do when dealing with an ongoing problem is tell ourselves we don't deserve to enjoy life because of the crisis we're dealing with.** It's as though we think we're unworthy of joy or that it would be irresponsible to be kind to ourselves while some crisis is going on.

"The truth is, it's exactly during crisis moments when we most need to be kind to ourselves. Otherwise, we will stay stuck in a negative state."

"Like having the parking brake on," I said.

"Exactly. What message are you sending your subconscious mind if you've convinced yourself you don't deserve to feel good?"

"Based on what you've taught me about the mind over the years, if I tell my subconscious I don't deserve to feel good, it will seek out thoughts and experiences that confirm this belief. And those thoughts and experiences probably aren't going to be very pleasant."

Eddie smiled. "No, they're not."

"This makes me think I've probably fed some pretty negative instructions into my subconscious over the past year. And sure enough, things just keep going bad for me. I feel stuck in a rut."

"In a very real sense, you *have* been stuck in a rut; a rut that you created with ongoing negative thoughts. You've likely developed a negative neural pathway in your mind that is looking for more negativity. You've programmed your mind to seek out experiences and thoughts that confirm the belief that you're not worthy of success or joy right now.

**"You're waiting for your circumstances to change before you give yourself permission to feel good again, but it doesn't work like that. You need to change your mindset first. You must choose to be positive and happy *in spite of* your circumstances. You need to allow yourself to feel**

**good first—to reprogram your mind to seek joy and success—***before* **you're going to start experiencing the positive results and circumstances you desire.**

"This is one of the most important secrets to a good life. **Don't wait on outside circumstances to change your attitude. Change your attitude first and you'll be surprised at how quickly your circumstances start to change.**

"When you feel good about yourself and you are excited about life, you're going to perform better. You're going to think with more clarity. You're going to find solutions much faster.

"The good news is, you can reprogram the ruts in your mind and you can do so fairly quickly. You've already started the process tonight by letting go of the negative thoughts and emotions you've been holding on to.

"I've got a few more techniques that work just as powerfully for feeling good again."

# 12

As I listened with anticipation, I was reminded what a wise and generous man Eddie Collins was and how much I had missed talking with my old friend over the past year. Why do we have a tendency to hunker down and pull away from others when life gets hard? I could have used Eddie's wisdom months ago, but I had retreated too far into a self-made bunker of anger and self-pity to really listen to him—or anyone else for that matter.

"Gratitude is the next key to feeling good again," Eddie said. "There's a reason I bring this up *after* showing you how to let go of all the negative emotions you've been holding on to.

"When you're angry, panicked, or grieving, it's natural to recoil when someone suggests thinking of things to be thankful for. You just don't want to hear it at that moment. But once you've been able to take a step back from the urgency of the situation and release some of the negative feelings you've been consumed by, thinking of things to be grateful for is one of the fastest and most powerful ways to shift your mindset from negative to positive.

"You've probably heard it said that you can't be grateful

and fearful at the same time. This is because when you are thinking of things to be grateful for, your mind is focused on positive things in the present. When you are thinking of things you fear, your mind is focused on negative things in the future. These mental pathways are moving in different directions.

"You can say the same thing about gratitude and anger. Gratitude focuses your mind on positive things in the present. Anger focuses your mind on negative things in the past. Again, completely different mental pathways.

"Our most destructive thoughts can usually be traced back to anger or fear. That's what makes gratitude so powerful. It's an emotion that sends your mind in a distinctly different direction from anger and fear—the two foundations of negative thinking.

"**The moment you force your mind to focus on gratitude is the moment you take away any control anger or fear had on you. It's the moment you ensure you have shifted your mind from a negative mental state to a positive mental state.**

"Choosing to be grateful for something is easy to do once you've let go of the panic and reminded yourself you don't have to stay focused on whatever negative thoughts have been forcing their way into your mind.

"All you have to do is make a mental list of things to be grateful for. You can write them down if you want, some people get more out of that, but you don't have to and you might not always be able to in the moment. The key is to think—really think—about some things you are grateful for. Meditate on them if you're in a quiet place and able to.

"I don't have to tell you all the things you have to be grateful for. They're easy to find once you tell your mind to start looking for them. Your wife, your kids, the air you breathe, the weather, the ability to see, to think, to feel, on and on this list could go."

"I know," I said. "I know I have so many things to be grateful for. I need to remind myself to think about them more."

Eddie nodded. "It requires discipline. Take time to do it every morning when you wake up and every night before you fall asleep. It only needs to take a minute or so, but no matter what else is going on or how many problems you're dealing with, you have to force your mind to focus on things to be grateful for. Once you start making a list, you'll keep thinking of more things to be grateful for. You'll start feeling like the luckiest guy in the world. Eventually, you'll start to realize what an ass you were being by complaining about so many things."

We both laughed.

"Right now, think about some things to be grateful for," Eddie said.

"Do I have to close my eyes again?"

"Only if you want to."

I smiled, looking up at the stars, and began thinking to

myself about how lucky I was to have a kind wife and hilarious kids who loved me no matter what my scorecard said. I thought about how lucky I was to be where I was right this moment, talking again to my childhood hero who had become a good friend and mentor. I appreciated being able to breathe in the night air in a country I loved, a country that had given me so many opportunities.

I took another deep breath—something that was becoming more and more frequent for me on this night, which was noteworthy considering how my breathing had been constrained by anger and stress for so long.

"The problems I'm dealing with," I said after a few moments of mental list-making, "they're not fun. But when I start thinking about it, I guess I have so many more things going *for* me than going against me."

"No guessing is necessary," Eddie said. "There's no doubt about it."

"I wish it was easier to think of these things in the heat of the moment, when I'm all stressed out and mad about something."

"It gets easier the more you do it. You just need to make it a habit. Like any other habit, it requires discipline and repetition. The more you do it, the more natural it will become for you."

# 13

Eddie and I spent the next hour or so discussing other ways for me to be kind to myself. He said my number one priority right now needed to be feeling good again.

"Only then can you start winning again," he said. "Nobody reaches their full potential in a state of anger, self-pity, or despair. Once you feel good again, you'll gain clarity, confidence, and hope."

Eddie told me how important it was to forgive whoever I was holding a grudge against.

"Holding on to grudges only hurts you," he said. "I assure you it's not hurting the other person."

He encouraged me to forgive the driver who ran into me. It was an accident. The guy surely feels awful about it. Move on. Eddie explained that holding a grudge would in no way make it easier to move past the accident; it would instead keep me tied to it, like that parking brake that won't let me drive freely.

He reminded me again that adversity was an unavoidable part of life. Problems were always going to come, but it would be a lot easier to deal with them if I accepted them as an inevitable part of life and didn't get mad or feel sorry for myself whenever I encountered them.

"Think of life as a game, and problems as challenges," Eddie said. "How boring would it be to play a game if your opponents always let you win or if you never had any obstacles to overcome? Where would be the fun or satisfaction in playing a game like that?

"Life is similar. If everything came easy, there would be no courage required, no perseverance required, no sacrifice required, no passion required, no faith or hope required. None of the character traits we all value so much would be necessary."

We also talked about golf. Eddie shared some of his favorite stories of playing the game he loved and asked me to do the same. I told him about rounds I played with my dad growing up. Fun stories from my playing days in college, my early days on the mini-tours, and my victories on the PGA Tour. He even got me to relive an exciting moment from just a few weeks ago in the first round of the Masters, when I birdied the opening hole.

Eddie finally had me smiling again about the game of golf.

"Your passion for the game is what fueled your success," Eddie said. "You've got to get that passion and joy back if you want to have success again."

I knew he was right. I had loved the game of golf since I was a kid. It had brought me so much joy and given me so many wonderful opportunities in life. I loved the sights, sounds, and smells of the game. I loved the challenges of each new hole, the beauty of the different courses, and the camaraderie with other golfers and fans.

"Don't resent the game you love because of what happened to you," Eddie said. "This is another way you are beating yourself up. You are focusing too much on what you don't like about the game instead of what you love about it.

"In your mind, you've turned the game into a source of fear instead of joy. You are focused on all the pressure and the obstacles instead of the pleasure and the opportunities. You have to shift your focus back to what you love about this game. Focus on things you appreciate about it. Focus on the joy being out on that course brings you. Allow yourself to once again *enjoy* this great game of ours.

"Let golf—something you have loved since you were a kid—be a refuge for you during tough times, not something to avoid. Don't resent the challenge of the game, which is one of the things that makes it so enjoyable for you. Embrace the challenge. Get excited about the challenge. Lose yourself in the challenge.

"Stop worrying so much about whether you keep your Tour card beyond this year. If this ends up being your final season on the Tour, why not squeeze every last ounce of joy out of it? What you focus on most will tend to come about. So, why not focus on the joy and pleasure of playing?

"Remember, Jack, it *is* a game. It's supposed to be fun.

Stop taking it so seriously."

Finally, as we rolled past 10 o'clock, Eddie shared one more key to being kind to myself.

"Before you call it a night, I've got an assignment for you," he said. "It will take you about an hour and a half. Think you can handle it?"

I looked at my watch. "I'll give it a try."

Eddie stood up. "Follow me. I want to show you something."

He led me inside and to an area of his home I'd never seen before. We walked down a hallway and past his large office, where I noticed the walls were lined with books from floor to ceiling.

At the end of the hall, he opened a door and stepped down a few steps into a dark room with no windows. He turned on the lights and revealed a massive home theater with reclining leather chairs, lit-up movie posters on the walls, and one of those old-timey popcorn makers in the corner.

"Nice, Eddie."

"I love movies. Only the right kinds, though." He tapped his temple. "The movies that feed your mind the right thoughts. Grab a seat and kick back. Want some popcorn?"

"Sure," I said, sinking into the plush leather recliner and placing my drink in the built-in cupholder.

"One of the most important keys to feeling good about

yourself is allowing yourself to laugh," he said as he filled two bags with popcorn. "I get the sense you haven't been doing much laughing lately."

"Prior to tonight, not so much."

"Why do we do that to ourselves?" He handed me one of the popcorn bags and set his bag on another chair. He hit a button on the wall that powered on his theater system. "We take life so seriously. When things aren't going our way, we refuse to laugh. We convince ourselves it would be irresponsible to laugh during tough times, but laughter is one of the most helpful things we can do if we want to shift our mental state from negative to positive."

He turned his attention back to me. "Laughter releases endorphins, which are natural pain killers. Laughter strengthens your immune system. It relaxes your muscles and instantly relieves stress and anxiety. Studies show it protects your heart and lowers your blood pressure. No matter what is going on, it makes you feel good about yourself and it fights depression. It improves your memory and mental focus. It also keeps you humble. I've never met a happy person who couldn't laugh at himself.

"Jack, if they could bottle up laughter, I think it would be the most beneficial drug on the market. But the truth is, it's available to us all any time we want it, if we would just give ourselves permission to use it."

Eddie opened a door at the front of the theater room and walked into a room behind the big screen. I could hear him opening and closing something. The screen in front of me lit up and the lights in the theater dimmed as Eddie returned from the room and shut the door behind him, now holding a controller in his hand.

He took his seat as the lights continued to dim and he clicked a button on his remote. "For the next hour and a half, you and I are going to laugh like we're kids again and remember what we love so much about our great sport."

And with that, the movie he picked began to play on the massive screen in front of us.

I took a handful of salty, buttery popcorn and watched as the screen flickered to life with the image of a night sky and I heard the familiar opening notes of the song "I'm Alright" by Kenny Loggins. I knew right then Eddie had chosen the 1980 golf comedy classic *Caddyshack* for the evening's feature presentation.

For the next 100 minutes, I did indeed laugh like I hadn't laughed in more than a year. Though I had seen the movie dozens of times in my younger days, it had been at least fifteen years since I last watched it. But just like most other avid golfers, I knew the movie by heart. As I watched all the hilarious scenes play out on that country club golf course, it did indeed remind me how much I enjoyed this beautiful, heartbreaking, challenging, cruel, serious, silly, sentimental, ridiculous, comforting, hilarious, and just-plain-*fun* game I had fallen in love with as a kid.

# 14

I woke up the next morning in Eddie's guesthouse. My first thought brought a smile to my face as I remembered Bill Murray delivering some of his hilarious lines from the movie Eddie and I had watched the night before. This was striking because most mornings since the accident, my first thoughts upon waking would make my stomach drop. Thoughts like, *Why did this happen to me? Why couldn't things go back to the way they used to be? What else will go wrong today?*

As I showered and got ready for the day, some of those negative thoughts came back to me. As much as last night's conversation and movie improved my mood, just as Eddie had warned, those persistent thoughts of anger, self-pity, and despair weren't finished with me.

I reminded myself to use the techniques Eddie taught me. I imagined negative thoughts dissipating in front of me or floating away. I took a couple of minutes to think about things to be grateful for. I recalled a few funny scenes from the movie, which made me chuckle out loud.

*Baby steps,* I thought to myself. *This is going to take time and discipline.*

"It's a beautiful day," Eddie said when I walked into his kitchen, the delicious smell of frying bacon in the air. He was making breakfast for Debbie and had set a place at the table for me as well. "Hope you like bacon and eggs."

"Absolutely," I said.

"Fuel for our round of golf this morning."

In the past whenever I visited Eddie, we would spend the next day playing golf together on his world-class course. I had not planned to do that this time.

"Actually, Eddie, I've got to book a flight out of here and get back to …"

Eddie and Debbie both looked at me, waiting for me to continue.

"… I guess I haven't decided exactly where I'm going next," I said.

Normally, I would be on my way to the site of the next PGA tournament. In this case, that would be the Charles Schwab Challenge in Fort Worth. However, I had flown into Austin planning to announce my retirement to Eddie and then head back to Kansas City to tell Ashley and our kids the same news.

After last night, I was rethinking my retirement plans.

"Perfect," Eddie said. "We'll play a morning round while you decide. Nothing soothes the mind like fresh air on a golf course."

# 15

Once again, Eddie was right. The smell of fresh-cut grass, the feel of the morning breeze, the views of the gorgeous green fairways and beautiful Austin hills around us, it all brought peace to my senses. And the focus required to hit that little white ball again and again forced me to take a needed break from thinking about the career decision that had been weighing on me.

"I've been meaning to ask you," I said to Eddie as he drove our golf cart to the third-hole tee box, "your story last night about the back issues you were dealing with, how did you fix it?"

"Yours still bothering you?"

"It comes and goes. I haven't noticed it so far today, but some mornings it's really bad. I'll wake up so stiff and sore that a sneeze will just about debilitate me."

Eddie nodded as we rolled to a stop behind the tee box. "Interesting that it comes and goes, isn't it?"

"I'd say it's more frustrating than interesting."

We stepped out of the cart and walked to the back of it to grab our drivers from our golf bags.

"When my back was acting up, I met with a doctor who

suggested another surgery," Eddie said. "I didn't want to risk that just yet. I worked on specific exercises with a trainer and a physical therapist. I even went to a chiropractor. Everything I did would usually help me feel better momentarily, but nothing seemed to have a lasting effect. When you have that pain in your lower back, it affects everything else, especially your swing."

"I know all about that," I said, taking a practice swing and feeling a sharp discomfort in my lower left back right on cue.

"I met with three other doctors who all said they couldn't tell for sure what was causing the issue. Just aging and playing so much golf, they said. They suggested things like steroid injections and lots of Advil.

"Frustrated that I couldn't find a clear solution, I started reading about the mind-body connection. A friend recommended I read a book by this New York City doctor who specialized in back problems, a guy named John Sarno. I read his book. In it, he had some *interesting* theories." Eddie chuckled.

"I'm curious." I had stopped swinging my driver. Eddie had my full attention.

"He said that oftentimes—not every time, of course—but oftentimes, back pain is caused by our brains. His theory was that our brains sometimes send physical pain to our lower backs or other areas in order to keep our minds from dwelling on more traumatic emotional pain. That is, if we were dealing with a high level of emotional stress or repressed rage inside, the brain would try to distract us from the stress or rage by giving us a physical pain to deal with instead—and lower backs were the most common area for this pain to develop. He said it could happen even if the original cause of the pain was physical trauma. Your brain knew where to keep sending the pain.

"In a nutshell, his solution was to simply talk to your brain when you felt the pain. Tell it, 'I know what you're doing, I know you're trying to protect me from emotional pain, but I would rather deal with the emotional pain instead.' Acknowledging that you knew what your brain was trying to do took away its power to do it. Once you knew the tactic your brain was trying to use to shift your attention, it would stop doing it and allow you to deal with the emotional issue instead."

Eddie looked at me with a half-smile and a raised eyebrow, wondering if I was buying any of this. "I know it sounds pretty out there, but I knew others who said it worked and I figured it wouldn't hurt to try."

"And did it work?"

Eddie teed up his ball, took two practice swings, and then hit his ball dead center. With a satisfying *ping* it launched off the tee high and straight into the air, landing in the middle of the fairway.

He turned to me with a big smile. "If it didn't work, I would never have been able to keep swinging like that. And it was nearly thirty years ago when I learned about it."

I shook my head. "That is incredible."

"It didn't happen overnight. It took a couple weeks of really talking to myself. But my back gradually got better and better. Eventually, it hardly ever bothered me at all. Still comes up now and again, and I still talk to my brain, I tell it, 'I know what you're doing.'

"I'm telling you, Jack, this self-talk stuff is powerful. The more I study the mental side of things and implement what I learn, the more convinced I am of how powerful our minds really are."

I teed up my ball and took a practice swing of my own. I again felt a sharp soreness in the left side of my lower back.

*No time like the present to try this,* I thought to myself. *I know what you're trying to do by causing this back pain, but I would rather deal with my emotions. I can handle it.*

I took another practice swing and, believe it or not, my back felt better with this swing. The pain wasn't gone, but it had subsided substantially.

I took another swing to test it and could swear the pain I had been dealing with was even less.

Maybe it was all in my head. The placebo effect, perhaps. Or, simply the excitement of thinking I might have some control over the situation.

Whatever the reason, all I know is that I then hit the very best drive I had hit since my accident. Clean, slight fade that landed in the fairway, pain-free. A strong gust of wind was at my back and the fairway sloped downhill at the point my ball first landed, so that all helped—I admit that—but my ball didn't stop rolling until it was 315 yards in front of us in the middle of the fairway.

"I thought you said you could no longer hit it 300 since your accident," Eddie said.

"I couldn't," I said.

"Amazing how powerful this mental stuff is, isn't it?"

# 16

"If you don't mind me asking, what was the emotional baggage you think your brain was trying to redirect?" I said as we walked onto the third-hole green.

"I don't mind at all," Eddie said. "I was dealing with a lot of the same stuff you are dealing with, the stuff we *all* deal with—no matter our profession. The pressure of competition. The fear that my best days were behind me. The worry that my career had been too good to be true and I was due for a setback. The stress of not knowing what the future held. Like you, I had let my focus go to all those negative, cynical thoughts.

"Once I faced my destructive thoughts head-on, I was able to let them go and replace them with positive, empowering ones."

"I'm surprised you were struggling with so many negative thoughts after all the success you had and all those years you spent working on your mental game."

"Like I've always said, the war within your mind never stops. You can't let your guard down. You've got to constantly be on the lookout for negative thoughts slipping back in and taking the upper hand in this battle."

Hearing that even a legend like Eddie Collins had to deal with the same fears, doubts, and worries I was dealing with reminded me that *everyone* has to fight that inner battle within their minds. No matter how many tournaments you win, how much success you have, or how many pats on the back you get, negative thoughts are always trying to knock you off course.

Throughout our round that morning, Eddie encouraged me to focus on feeling good about myself. He didn't want me thinking about my future plans. He wanted me to let go and enjoy *playing* golf on this beautiful day.

I played a good round overall. Not spectacular, but considering the windy conditions we were dealing with, finishing 2 strokes under par on this difficult PGA-level course was a solid outing.

What was more important than my score was the realization that neither my back nor my knee gave me the late-round trouble it had been giving me since my comeback. Sure, I noticed the dull pain and tenderness here and there, and driving a cart instead of walking the course made a huge difference, but I couldn't help but think talking to myself the way Eddie encouraged was a big reason why the pain had subsided.

"I'm shocked at how much better I'm feeling," I said during our post-round lunch at the clubhouse. I twisted my trunk back and forth, something I couldn't do without sharp pains after previous rounds of golf this year. "I mean, this is really incredible. I can't believe self-talk can make that big of a difference that quickly."

"I'm surprised myself how good you're feeling," Eddie said. "It usually takes at least a couple of weeks before you start feeling *that* much better."

"Maybe my excitement is covering up the pain. I'm excited to know there is *something* that might work for me. *Something* I can do to turn things around and start playing better. I've been desperate for hope."

Eddie pointed at me. "That right there might be the single biggest key to a happy life. Hope.

"**Hope is a powerful thing. And I'm not talking about the passive, wishful-thinking type of hope that says, 'I hope something good comes along and makes my life better.' I'm talking about the active, take-control type of hope that says, 'I have the power to make my life better today.'**

"This is ultimately what the mental shift we've been talking about comes down to. It's a shift from helplessness to hopefulness, from feeling powerless to feeling powerful, from thinking about what you can't control to thinking about what you can.

"**Once you shift your mind to what you *can* control and how you *can* change your life—as opposed to focusing on the past or all the circumstances you can't control—that's when you regain your power.** That's the power of hope.

"When you make that mental shift, you'll instantly feel better about whatever problem you're dealing with. And when you start feeling better, you start playing better and living better. Good things start happening."

"Is this the part where you remind me that I always have control over two things: my effort and my attitude?"

Eddie laughed. "Sounds like I don't need to remind you."

I joined in with a smile and then sighed. "I know this stuff. I know what I *should* be doing. But it can be *so* hard to make that mental shift when everything is going wrong."

"Not if you remind yourself how much it *will* make a difference. Choosing to shift your mindset won't make you feel much better if you doubt whether it will make a difference in whatever you're dealing with. But if you *know* it will, you'll realize the importance of making that shift and making it quickly in order to turn things around.

"**Successful and happy people haven't cracked some secret code that allows them to avoid obstacles. They've mastered the art of responding to obstacles in the most positive way possible. They do this by choosing to believe they *can* improve their lives, no matter what has gone wrong. They choose to believe that though they might not be able to do anything about what has already happened, they *can* do plenty about what happens next.**

"That is what hope is. And hope is a very powerful mental state."

# 17

"Hope is something I've been lacking lately," I said.

"Clearly," Eddie said. "But at least something good has come out of your hopeless mental state."

"What's that?"

"It brought you here. It brought you to a rock-bottom moment where you felt compelled to fly out here and tell me you were going to do the thing people ultimately do when they lose their hope: Quit."

"Retire," I said with a sheepish grin.

Eddie ignored my correction. "I can see you're getting your hope back. You already look ten years younger than when you showed up at my doorstep yesterday. You look lighter, like the weight of the world is no longer bearing down on you. You look ... almost happy."

"I am feeling better. You're making me rethink my retirement plans. At the very least, I might as well play another tournament or two to see if I can get through an event without embarrassing myself."

Eddie grimaced. "That's not the commitment I was hoping to hear."

I chuckled. "Baby steps. I don't want to get ahead of

myself. Let's not forget how I was playing two days ago. I feel good today, but I've had plenty of good practice rounds over the last six months. Things can change in a hurry when the pressure turns up at an actual tournament."

Eddie shook his head. "That type of thinking won't get it done."

My smile faded. I thought my mentor would be happy to hear I had decided to play another tournament or two. Apparently, that wasn't enough.

"The first step in making the mental shift we're talking about is being kind to yourself and feeling good again," Eddie said. "That allows you to start thinking with more clarity.

"The second crucial step is completely eliminating the option to quit. **You must decide that quitting is not an option. There can be no retreat. There can be no Plan B.**

"When times get hard, you can't give yourself the option to quit. Don't even entertain the idea. Because let me tell you, if you allow even the thought that quitting might be for the best, it will only sound more enticing as new challenges come up.

"As we've talked about, feeling good about yourself and thinking positive again is important, but it's not going to make it so you hit nothing but fairways and greens from here on out—on the course or in any other area of your life. You will continue to face hardships. You will continue to be blindsided by obstacles. And the moment you face bigger adversity, that little thought about quitting can get a whole lot louder. You know what happens when a thought becomes more dominant."

"My life will move toward it."

"Exactly. That's why quitting can't even be an option in your mind. It can't be a safety net. You have to make a complete and total commitment to chasing your goal all the way and never surrendering."

I nodded as I finished up my sandwich, but Eddie must have seen something on my face that told him I wasn't totally buying what he was saying.

# 18

"What is it?" Eddie said.

I wiped my mouth with a napkin, crumpled it up, and tossed it onto my empty plate. "All the 'no retreat, no surrender, never back down' type of talk sounds great, and I know what I'm about to say sounds really negative, but let's be honest, there are times when you *have* to retire. There are times when the job you lose never comes back. There are times when the injury never quite heals. There are times when you come up short of your goal and you are forced to move on to something else. And during those times you better have a Plan B in mind."

Eddie lifted his finger. "Ah, but there's a key difference between adapting to changing conditions along the way and having a plan for retreating before you even get started.

"Every difficult goal is going to require adapting along the way. This happens on nearly every single hole we play on the golf course. When the ball doesn't end up exactly where we wanted it to, we have to adapt our original plan. That's part of the game. We don't decide to walk off the course just because our first shot lands in the woods.

"Imagine two players getting ready to play a round of

golf. One player tells himself, 'If this front nine doesn't go my way, I'm going to call it a day at the turn and go home.' The other player tells himself, 'I paid for a full round and no matter what happens I'm going to play a full eighteen holes today.' One player has told himself if the going gets tough, he's out of there. The other has made a commitment to see it all the way through no matter how tough it gets. Which player do you think is more likely to finish the full round of golf?"

"Obviously, the second player. But that's different. I'm talking about real life here, not a round of golf."

"It's all the same to your mind," Eddie said. "When you give your subconscious a specific goal, it will do everything it can to help you reach that goal. If you give it a goal along with an option to retreat and do something deemed *easier* if the going gets tough, it will move you towards the easier option as soon as you encounter too many challenges. It's your mind's way of hitting the bailout button when things get tough. Don't give your mind the option to push that button in the first place."

"You don't think having a Plan B is *ever* a good idea?"

"I'm fine with giving yourself a set time to reevaluate your plans and life goals. The entrepreneur might have to tell himself, 'I will give myself one year to get this business off the ground and if it isn't turning a profit by then, I will reevaluate my career choice.' The wannabe author might tell herself, 'I'll give myself three years to chase this dream and if I haven't published a book by then, I will reevaluate.' In your case, you might have to tell yourself, 'I will give myself until the end of this season and if I haven't played well enough to keep my Tour card, I will reevaluate my next career move then.'

"The key is to not even entertain the idea of bailing on your goal until that set date occurs. Otherwise, you'll always be thinking about what Plan B might look like, what might happen if your original plan doesn't work out, when it might be time to call it quits. Those thoughts run directly counter to your primary objective, which is to give it everything you've got to make your original goal successful."

"Put any alternate plans off to a later time?" I said.

"Exactly. If you start to worry, tell yourself you'll deal with it when the set date comes up, but not until then. You simply can't operate at your best if you've given your mind two opposing destinations. You must have one dominating goal in mind. No retreat. No surrender.

"To be clear, altering your course along the way is part of the process. You might have to take new routes along the way, but the destination you have in mind should not change. When you start thinking about a different destination, that's when you're in trouble.

"Plans will be altered. I might have to find a new way to get to where I want to be, but I will not give myself an option to stop heading towards the one destination I've given my mind.

**"When times get hard and it seems like your original plan is no longer working, ask yourself, 'If quitting on my dream is *not* an option, what do I need to do differently?'** You will come up with clear, productive answers. Answers that are much different than what you'd get if you told yourself it was okay to quit on your dream entirely.

"When I started my career as a pro golfer, I obviously knew if I couldn't win and I ran out of money, I would have to find another line of work. What that work would be I wasn't really sure. I figured the time to make a new plan—to choose a new destination—would be when I had exhausted all other options in trying to achieve my goal of making it as a pro golfer.

"I understood that a day would come when life would tell me it was time to dream a new dream. But until that day came, I would not feed my mind a new goal. I would not entertain the idea of a new destination until I had no other choice.

"In your case right now, if retiring is not an option—if you don't allow yourself to even *think* about doing it—you'll notice that your mind will be forced to find a way to succeed despite the obstacles you're dealing with. It will become obsessed with figuring out new solutions to your problems and finding a way to keep you on the Tour because that's the only goal you're allowing it to seek.

"This goes back to the power of focus. **You can't give yourself two opposing goals. If you allow your mind to**

**believe quitting is a reasonable option, you are essentially giving it a goal that is directly opposed to what you really want. Your mind will then change its focus from one goal to the other depending on what you're experiencing at any given moment.**

"When things are going well as you pursue your dream, your mind will stay focused on achieving that dream. But the moment you face a major obstacle in your path, it will start focusing on the path of retreat, the other 'goal' you gave it.

"**You've got to go *all in* on your dream destination. You can't have one foot in and one foot out.** You can't move forward very efficiently if you've always got an eye out for the nearest exit when things get hard.

"When you study the very highest achievers—from great athletes to artists to business owners and all types of top professionals—you will often hear them say they wouldn't be where they are if they had ever given themselves the option to do something else. They say they would have never made it through the hard times if they had the option to quit. When it comes to chasing a really big dream in life, those who have another option usually end up taking it when the going gets tough.

"William James, the father of American psychology, famously said, 'It is our attitude at the *beginning* of a difficult task which, more than anything else, will affect its successful outcome.' It's difficult to have a winning attitude if you are making plans for retreating before you even get started.

"That's why I feel so strongly that you must eliminate the option to quit. Don't even think about it.

"If you're going to play this game, you have to play it to the hilt. You should have one goal and one goal only, and that is to succeed at the highest level. That's the only thing you should be thinking about.

"**You can't be your best if you've got a bailout plan in the back of your mind. You have to give your mind one option and one option only.**

"Eventually, you're correct, life will tell you it's time to retire, to move on to something else, to dream another dream. And when that day comes, you'll figure out what to do next, what new dream to dream. But that day is not to-day. And thinking about it now will only confuse your mind and prevent you from staying focused on what you really want to achieve.

"Jack, you've got to tell yourself right now that quitting is not an option. Retirement is not an option. Retreat is not an option. **When you give your mind one path and one path only, it will find a way to get you there in the fastest and most effective way possible. Let it do its job. Eliminate all other options.**"

# 19

I needed some time to think about what Eddie had said. I took a quiet walk on a nearby nature trail he suggested.

As I made my way along the trail, the huge trees on both sides of me swaying back and forth on this windy afternoon, I thought about something I had not acknowledged before. Since my accident—all through the rehab, the training, and the practice rounds as I worked towards my comeback—the dominant thought in my mind had constantly been, *We'll see how this goes.* Somedays, when things were going well, I was optimistic about my comeback. Other days, when I wasn't feeling well or playing well, I surrendered to the idea that this wasn't going to work.

How could I expect to achieve such a difficult goal if I wasn't 100-percent committed to making it happen?

Eddie was right. I had one foot in and one foot out.

From the start of my comeback journey, I had serious doubts about whether I could get back to the physical state I was in prior to the accident. Should I really be surprised that I had failed at this comeback when I was constantly thinking about what I might have to do when my golf career ended?

"If you're going to do this, you need to be all in," Eddie had said just before I left for my walk.

That thought ran through my mind over and over as I walked along the trail, breathing in the fresh air and listening to the leaves bristle in the wind.

Was I willing to go *all* in?

Was I willing to eliminate every single thought of doing something else?

Was I willing to set one goal and one goal only? Was I willing to go after that goal with *everything* I had?

What was holding me back from fully committing to this goal? I had to admit the answer was fear.

But why? Why was I afraid to go all in?

I think it was the fear of failing and then not knowing what to do next. I wanted a safety net in mind, something to save me if this comeback attempt faltered. But like Eddie wisely pointed out, if the day came when I had to do something else, I could figure out what to do *then*. Thinking about failing prior to trying was only going to prevent me from being my best in the moment.

When I finished my walk, I pulled out my phone and dialed Mike's number.

He answered on the first ring, as though he was waiting for my call. "Hey Jack, what's the word?"

"Can you meet me in Fort Worth tomorrow?"

"I already booked my ticket. I knew Eddie would talk some sense into you."

"No more waffling on this comeback," I said. "No more seeing how I feel once I get out there. We're doing this thing. I am *all in*."

"Now that's the big brother I grew up with!"

# 20

After talking to Mike, I called Ashley and told her I wouldn't be coming home as I thought I might.

"It's time for me to get serious about winning again," I said.

She could hear the intensity in my voice, the renewed commitment to my dream.

"I am so glad to hear you say this," she said.

Ashley handled the travel itinerary for my life on the Tour. She told me my best option at this point was to rent a car and make the three-hour drive from Austin to Fort Worth. The drive helped me further clarify my goals and refocus on once again being the best player I could possibly be.

No more waffling back and forth on this comeback attempt. No more one foot in, one foot out. No more retirement talk. No more feeling it out and hoping for the best.

I had to go all in on this renewed dream.

I was *determined* to make a triumphant return to the sport I loved.

Mike and I spent the next three days practicing in Fort Worth. I focused on being kind to myself and anytime thoughts of anger, fear, or failure wormed their way into my mind, I shut them down using the visualization technique Eddie taught me. It was amazing how well it worked the more I did it.

When I teed off at the Charles Schwab Challenge on Thursday morning, I felt like a new man from the start. I bombed my opening drive 315 yards (aided by the wind and a long downhill bounce on the dry fairway grass), chose not to lay up and reached the green with a 265-yard approach shot, and sank a 15-foot putt to eagle the Par 5 first hole.

As we walked off the green, Mike pulled me close and said with a smile, "Where has that been this season?"

I laughed back. "Amazing what a little shift in perspective can do."

Now, I wish I could tell you that from that opening hole on I played a flawless tournament culminating with me hoisting the first-place trophy and taking my picture with one of those giant cardboard checks on Sunday afternoon. However, that's not the reality of the situation.

At the end of the first round, I was 3 strokes under par. I gave 2 of those strokes back on Friday, but did manage to make the cut by 1 stroke. That marked the first time since my return to the Tour that I was playing on Saturday and Sunday.

I finished the tournament 2 strokes under par and tied for thirty-sixth place. My performance didn't make any headlines, but it did give me some much-needed confidence and squelch any questions from reporters about my impending retirement.

The back pain I had been dealing with was better, but far from nonexistent. During the back nine of each round, I felt it getting sorer. It wasn't so bad that it forced me to alter my swing to avoid pain—like it had in previous outings—but it was still annoying.

I continued talking to myself whenever I noticed it.

*I know what you're doing,* I said to my brain, *and I don't need you redirecting my emotions. I can handle the pressure.*

It wasn't some magical cure, but it did seem to help each time I did this.

Interestingly, it was my short game that caused me more problems during the tournament. I missed a handful of putts in the 5-to-6-foot range, a range where a Tour pro should be making at least 75-percent of his putts. And on the 18th hole Sunday, my nerves got the best of me as I came up a good two inches short on a 7-foot putt, which cost me about $20,000 in lost earnings.

I had a long way to go, but making the cut and playing a full four rounds for the first time since my return to the Tour was a cause for celebration.

# 21

I traveled to Dublin, Ohio, the following week to play in the Memorial Tournament, one of the PGA Tour's "signature events," as they are called. These tournaments aren't as big as the four Majors, but they come with purses more than twice as large as most other PGA events and the pressure gets turned up.

I knew this tournament was going to be a big test. Was the previous week a fluke? Did I benefit from competing against a field of players that didn't include as many of the game's top names—those who would surely be competing at the Memorial? Was I riding high on adrenaline after Eddie renewed my hope; perhaps that was why my back had not bothered me as much? Would that adrenaline fade? Would I be able to handle the increased pressure that came with a signature event like this one?

Those were the doubts creeping into my mind as I flew to Ohio on Monday morning.

My kids had just finished their school year and Ashley had planned months ago to bring them to this tournament. We rented a nice house near the Muirfield Village Golf Club, where the tournament would be played.

Our plan was to mix work and play for a week. The kids could start their summer vacation with a fun trip and I could enjoy hanging out with them at the end of each day. It was supposed to be a great way for me to spend some extra time with my family during a busy summer of traveling on the Tour. However, I wasn't taking advantage of the moment the way I hoped.

We had a nice evening on Monday, but during my Tuesday practice round, I wasn't focused. My mind was all over the place, and so was my golf ball. I played poorly, missing fairway after fairway on my drives.

My swing had a natural fade to it. I always adjusted my shots accordingly. But on this afternoon, it was pushing farther to the right than normal, completely missing fairways. My fade had become a slice.

*What now?* I thought to myself. It wasn't enough that my putting had struggled in the previous tournament, now it was also my drives and mid-range shots. It was like I developed a new twitch I couldn't control in the middle of my swing, which caused me to miss the sweet spot of my clubface when I connected with the ball. I only missed by a fraction, but that fraction was making my ball end up all over the place. I couldn't figure out what was causing this latest issue. Mike offered suggestions, but nothing seemed to help.

After my frustrating afternoon on the course, I was agitated that I had to rush to the rental house to be on time for dinner with my family, as I had promised. During dinner, I quietly stewed about my erratic swing instead of giving Ashley and the kids quality attention. Not exactly Dad of the Year behavior.

Ashley knew something was wrong. I told her I was sorry, but I needed to head back to the course to work on my swing. She smiled and told me it was no problem. She knew how I was when I got in these moods. She knew I needed some quiet time to get my anxious mind under control more than I needed an extra hour or two of working on my swing.

I drove to a nearby driving range. Though the sun had set, this range was lit up, which would allow me to work on my swing as long as needed—or at least until the range closed. The range had a long line of hitting bays and there were only a few other golfers using them, which was nice to see. I picked a hitting bay on the far end, hoping I wouldn't have to talk to anyone as I tried to fix my swing and ease my mind with shot after shot.

Half an hour into this ritual, I was still struggling to quiet my mind. Intrusive, negative thoughts kept attacking.

*You're not ready for this big of an event.*

*Is that your back hurting again? Just wait until you have to walk seventy-two holes this weekend.*

*Why am I pushing my ball so far to the right? I was hitting the fairways fine on Sunday. What the hell changed over the past forty-eight hours to cause this?*

*It's ALWAYS something. Just when I think I've got things figured out ...*

After two solid shots that landed right where I wanted them to, I fired a shot into the night sky and watched my ball slice farther and farther and *farther* to the right. I exhaled in frustration.

"You've always had a strong fade," I heard a familiar voice say behind me.

I turned around to see Eddie grinning big as he walked towards the empty bay just to the left of mine, his golf bag slung over his right shoulder and his left hand gripping the handle of a large bucket of balls.

For a second, I thought my mind was playing tricks on me. "Eddie, how did you know I was here?"

He tapped his temple. "The power of the mind."

"Sure," I said with a chuckle.

He placed his bag on its stand and his bucket of balls in the designated opening between us. "I tried your phone, but you weren't answering. Called Ashley, she checked your GPS and told me where you were. I figured I'd surprise you."

"Did she tell you I was having another one of my freakouts?"

Eddie pulled his driver out of his bag. "She didn't put it quite so bluntly, but I got the message you didn't have your best practice round today."

I nodded. "You didn't need to come all this way."

"I'm staying just a few miles away. Debbie and I finished dinner; I figured I'd stop by and see how my protégé was feeling."

Eddie attended this tournament every year. The Memorial was hosted by his good friend and fellow golf legend Jack Nicklaus.

"I'm not having the best day," I said. "My ball was all over the place this afternoon. I can't figure out what I'm doing wrong. And when that happens, that negative chatter gets going in my mind again. Just when I think I'm back on track, life seems to be telling me, 'Not so fast.'"

"I'm not surprised," Eddie said. "Truth is, I was planning to talk with you about something important before this next tournament started.

"That strategy I told you about for shifting your mind during tough times, I haven't shared half of it with you. Being kind to yourself and eliminating the option to quit—those are only the first steps."

He reached into his bucket of golf balls and placed a half-dozen or so on the green mat he was standing on. He teed one up, took his stance, then two practice swings. His swing might not have had the start-to-finish grace it once did. It now had some awkward, age-induced hitches. Every time he swung away, it looked to me like he might lose his balance, but he never did. He had adjusted to the hitches to ensure he was still making consistent, dead-center contact with the ball.

Eddie stepped forward and swung away, connecting with that piercing *ping* sound that let you know he made perfect contact. His golf ball launched into the night air, high and straight. Not near as far as he once hit it, of course, but his ball undoubtedly would have landed in the middle of the fairway if we were on a course.

Eddie looked at me with a smile. "Ready for the next lesson?"

# 22

Eddie Collins was known as one of the game's greatest "ball strikers" ever. This refers to a golfer who is extremely consistent when he makes contact with the ball. He connects in the sweet spot, dead center of his clubface, again and again. Ben Hogan, Tiger Woods, Lee Trevino, Jack Nicklaus, Eddie Collins—it's a thing of beauty to watch these legendary ball strikers swing with such consistency, to hit the ball so clean over and over again.

Here I was, getting to watch one of those legends in person. Despite the hitches he had developed with age, he *still* found the perfect sweet spot with remarkable consistency.

Not all great ball strikers were necessarily long off the tee, but what they lacked in distance they would make up for with control. Eddie told me three years ago that from a young age he learned to sacrifice distance for direction. He cared much more about where on the course his ball landed than how far it went.

He once admitted that in today's era, when guys are bombing it farther than ever, his skillset might not have been as successful.

I told him I wasn't so sure about that. Though he had

never been the longest driver, Eddie was great at putting the ball right where he needed it off the tee, hitting fairways around 70-percent of the time throughout most of his career. And—like all of the game's greatest players—he was also a master of the short game and getting out of trouble when his ball *didn't* land where he wanted it to.

"Maybe you're right, I probably would've been just fine," the smiling winner of forty-nine PGA events and seven Majors told me with a wink and a grin back then.

On this night, I watched him hit a few more balls and had to shake my head at his consistency. Here I was, almost forty years younger than him, whacking the ball all over the place, searching for consistent contact. And here he was: high and straight, high and straight, again and again. He smiled approvingly as his latest ball landed, then turned his attention to me.

"Being kind to yourself is the first step to shifting your mind from helpless to hopeful," Eddie said. "Eliminating the option to quit removes distractions and forces you to focus on being the best you can be. But those two steps aren't enough to complete the shift you need to make, especially after such a traumatic setback and the time you've spent ruminating about it."

He placed another ball on his tee and swung again. This time, for the first time this evening, he missed his sweet spot just a bit and his ball pulled slightly left.

"It's easy to slip right back into your old way of

thinking," Eddie said as he stepped back and looked at me again. "After all, you've been conditioning your mind to seek out negative confirmations. Your subconscious is looking for ways to confirm your doubts about whether you'll ever be able to play at the level you did before. It's looking for ways to confirm your doubts about whether any of this mental stuff actually helps. Your default mindset lately has been to doubt yourself instead of believe in yourself. That bias is not going to go away overnight.

"In times like this, you need to get back to the fundamentals of your mental game."

"The fundamentals?"

"That's right. The essentials. The things that make the *biggest* impact in the way you think. Things you know you should be paying attention to, but may have gotten lackadaisical about.

"When your physical game is off, you go back to the physical fundamentals. You pay closer attention to your grip, your stance, your tempo. You analyze what you're doing differently, right? Well, it's the same thing for your mental game.

"When you find yourself agitated or worried—when negative thoughts get louder than normal—ask yourself if you've lost sight of the fundamentals. In almost every instance, you have.

"That's the third step in this mental shift process: get back to the fundamentals. Focus on the things that make the *biggest* impact in your thinking.

"When you find yourself struggling with intrusive negative thoughts, go back to the fundamentals and you will get back on track."

Eddie fired another shot into the sky, this one back to his high-and-straight ways. As he watched his ball land, he gave a slight nod of satisfaction.

"Is this the part where you remind me how important my self-image is?" I said. "Because I already know that. You've been telling me for years how I'll never be able to outperform my self-image, how it's the foundation for everything else.

"The problem is, when your world gets turned upside down the way mine has, your self-image becomes very brittle. The slightest setback makes me question all my old beliefs. Anytime something goes wrong, I start thinking it will never get better. I *know* how important my self-image is. The problem is my self-image is not in a good place right now."

Eddie placed both hands on the top of his driver, leaning on it slightly as he faced me.

"That is why it's so important to get back to the fundamentals," he said. "To get back to a positive mental state and rebuild your self-image, you have to actually *do* the things that will get you there. Knowing what you need to do is much different than actually *doing* what you need to do. That's where discipline comes in. You have to commit to practicing the fundamentals in order to see the results you desire."

"And what exactly are these fundamentals you keep talking about?"

"Over the past forty years or so, **I've learned the two most important things you need to practice daily if you want to stay in a positive mental state are feeding your mind positive material and protecting your mind from negative material.** That's it. Those are the two essentials. When you feel overwhelmed or distracted, go back to those two things and you'll get back on track.

"**If you're not doing those two things consistently throughout the day, you can't be surprised if you're suffering through mood swings, doubting yourself, or feeling agitated and worried. You can't be surprised your self-image is brittle if you're not actively feeding your mind the positive and protecting it from excessive negativity.**

"You have to feed your mind positive thoughts and positive visions for your future. You also have to protect it from the many negative things constantly trying to bombard it. You have to feed it positive self-talk instead of listening to whatever negative thoughts happen to bubble up.

"Just like mastering physical habits—like your daily training regimen or your pre-swing routine—mastering the mental fundamentals requires discipline. You have to be disciplined about how you feed and protect your mind."

# 23

"I think I've heard this before," I said with a smile, acknowledging the advice Eddie had given me over the years.

"Indeed, you have," Eddie said. "But are you practicing these things? Are you actually *doing* the things you know you should be doing every day?"

"Not like I used to. I did make a point to think about what I'm grateful for after we talked last week. I was pretty consistent about it for a few days. But then I got sidetracked. Too busy, I suppose. Too many other things in my head. Maybe I felt like I didn't need to keep doing it *every* day."

"Feeding and protecting your mind needs to become a consistent habit. It's got to be something you commit to every single day.

**"When you get up in the morning, the first thing you need to do is say something positive to yourself. Something like, 'I'm going to make today a great day. I'm excited for what's ahead!'**

"I know it sounds cheesy, but it works. It sets the tone for the day. It tells your mind who is in charge and the direction you want your thoughts to go.

"Continue this type of empowering self-talk as you get

ready for the day.

"Once you have some time to sit and think, spend a minute thinking about things you're grateful for and another minute or two visualizing things you want to achieve. This doesn't take long. Allow yourself to *feel* the emotions associated with your thoughts of gratitude and visions of success. Rev up some excitement. **How you start your day makes a huge impact on what kind of day you end up experiencing.**

"Then, all through the day, continue to feed yourself empowering messages like, 'I feel great. I am lucky. I am blessed. Things are going my way. I can achieve anything I put my mind to.' Those types of thoughts."

"I've tried that," I said. "Earlier this season, I kept telling myself, 'I feel great,' but it wasn't helping. In fact, saying it just made me angrier."

"You were in such a negative mental state, you couldn't believe what you were saying. If you are in that type of state, try simply saying, 'I'm getting better and better.' You might not be where you want to be, but you can always tell yourself you're getting *closer* to where you want to be. That simple change in perspective can be enough to break out of a negative state."

"I'll try it."

"Make sure you do. And don't wait for something bad to happen before you feed yourself empowering messages. In difficult moments, when your emotions are raw, it can feel phony or forced to repeat positive phrases if it isn't the way you normally talk to yourself. But if you make it a point to give yourself empowering messages throughout the day, it will be a lot easier to believe those messages when you need them most—during moments of adversity.

"At the end of the night, again take some time to be grateful and to visualize positive outcomes for the future. Then, read something positive. This is one of the best things you can do for your mindset. The last thing you feed your mind before you fall asleep tends to sink into your subconscious, so make sure you're giving it something positive, something inspiring.

"Have you been doing these things, Jack?"

"Not consistently."

"It's got to be a habit. It's got to become your *normal* way of thinking, not the exception that you call on only when times get tough.

"And what about the type of material you're consuming? Have you been protecting your mind from negative news programs lately? Have you been monitoring the things you watch or listen to, making sure they aren't encouraging cynical, fearful, or helpless beliefs?"

I thought about how I had listened to a popular podcast on my flight the day before. The host and his guest spent two hours talking about the negative direction this world is headed in, all the things going wrong, all the people who were corrupting our society. It was entertaining, for sure, but I was now being reminded how unhealthy it was to be listening to those messages, especially when I was in such a brittle mental state.

After Eddie began mentoring me three years ago, I made it a habit to protect my mind from too much negative noise. But I got lazy about it. I let my guard down. Even before my accident, I had become less diligent about what I was allowing myself to listen to or watch during off hours, especially while traveling.

Why did I do that? I couldn't say for sure. I suppose I simply stopped thinking it mattered all that much. I told myself I could handle it, that it was no big deal here and there. But, like a car wreck you pass on the road, it's hard to look away from negative, sensationalized news. It grabs your attention. And once you start giving it your attention, it keeps pulling you back for more.

"I'm not saying you need to bury your head in the sand and avoid all news," Eddie said, "but you need to be aware of the type of messages you're inundating your mind with. Messages from the news are often about the worst in society. Many movies, shows, and music paint extremely negative images of the world.

"I know it isn't possible to avoid all cynical messages. But at the very least, when you're exposing yourself to them, you better make sure you're countering them with positive messages that outweigh the negative. That means watching and listening to material that makes you laugh or feel empowered. Feed your mind stories about the great things people are achieving.

"You can't be neutral about this. I once read a study that said as much as ninety-percent of the messages the average person is exposed to each day are negative. On top of that, as humans we have a natural tendency to pay more attention to the negative messages. They have a greater impact on us; they stick with us longer and invoke a greater emotional response. When you recognize this, you understand why it's so hard to stay in a positive mental state if you aren't proactively protecting your mind from excessive negativity.

"Did you know that medical students who specialize in the study of a specific disease have a tendency to develop the symptoms of that same disease?"

"Seriously?" I said with a raised eyebrow.

"Seriously." Eddie nodded. "They've done studies on it. It's truly amazing how powerful the mind is, and even more amazing how unaware most people are of its power.

"I'll say it again: your life moves in the direction of your most dominant thoughts. That's not a theory. That's a fact. So, you better make sure *you* are deciding what your dominant thoughts are."

# 24

Eddie loved talking about the power of the mind and his excitement was contagious.

The more Eddie taught me these things, the more I realized *I* had the power to change my circumstances. I *could* change my life by taking control of my thinking.

"When we realize how important these simple fundamentals are, we have to ask ourselves why we're not implementing them," Eddie said, then waited for me to respond.

"I could tell you I'm too busy," I said, "but I know *everybody* is busy."

"Exactly," Eddie said. "You can always make time for the things you know you need to do. When you're brushing your teeth, when you're driving somewhere, when you're doing a thousand other mindless things you do every day, you can make the effort to feed your mind positive messages."

"I could tell you I'm mentally strong enough to not let negative messages affect me, but based on what I know about the subconscious and how it takes in everything it's exposed to, I know that's not true either."

"Right again. The subconscious is constantly accepting

whatever message you feed it—good or bad—and what you feed the inner affects the outer. Feed it cynical messages repeatedly and you'll adopt cynical beliefs about what you're capable of achieving. As they say, 'garbage in, garbage out.'"

"I can make the time and I know the power of the subconscious," I said. "Here's why I think it's easy to fall away from the fundamentals. When things were going well, I didn't think I needed to keep working them because I thought I had it all figured out. And when things were going bad, I started doubting whether this stuff ever worked in the first place."

Eddie could see he was getting through to me. "Life is showing you just how necessary it is to keep practicing the fundamentals. Without them, everything else falls apart.

"**You can't be neutral in your approach to the mental game. You have to take responsibility. You have to focus on the fundamentals: feeding your mind positive material and protecting it from too much negative material.**

"If you do those two things and you do them throughout each day, you're going to see positive changes in your life.

"But just like mastering the physical fundamentals, the mental fundamentals require discipline on your part. *Daily* discipline. It must become a habit.

"You have to *make* the time and effort to feed your mind positive material.

"You have to make the decision to protect yourself from too many negative messages—even if those messages are entertaining or seem like no big deal.

"You have to take control of your self-talk. Too many people believe whatever thought floats into their head is something they need to address right that moment. Wrong. *You* are in control. You can let it float away. You can choose to focus on something else.

"Like everything else in life, it all comes down to your choices.

"You get to choose whether to dwell on negative thoughts or let them float away harmlessly. You get to choose whether to repeat positive affirmations throughout the day or decide such things are silly. You get to choose whether to visualize every shot before you take it or rush through your routine.

"Jack, *you* get to choose whether to take the mental fundamentals just as seriously as the physical fundamentals. Don't discount their effectiveness. You've seen firsthand how well you play and how well your life goes when you take your mental training seriously. You've also seen what happens when you don't."

# 25

Eddie and I spent the next half-hour going over the physical fundamentals of my golf swing.

"Whenever my swing acts up," Eddie said, "I go back to the fundamentals first. My grip, my stance, my tempo. Usually, the problem can be found in one of those three things. And if one of those is off, there is usually a mental reason for why I have subconsciously made the change."

"It always goes back to the mental game with you, doesn't it?" I said.

"Always."

After some helpful evaluation, we agreed my tempo was inconsistent. I was swinging harder than normal. Trying too hard. Mike had thought the same thing earlier in the afternoon.

But Eddie being Eddie, he wanted to find the root cause—the mental cause. He believed I was swinging harder because I was anxious about the increased pressure this week. The pressure to prove the previous tournament was a turning point for my comeback and the pressure to prove I could play well when the competition increased at a PGA signature event.

"I can tell you all the reasons why you can compete with anyone this weekend," Eddie said. "But that's not going to do you near as much good as you telling yourself those reasons. You have to take control of your self-talk. You have to repeat empowering messages to yourself until you believe them."

By the end of our practice session, I was striking the ball with better consistency and feeling confident again.

Before falling asleep that evening, I made sure to think of how grateful I was for my family, for Eddie's kindness, and for the opportunity to still be playing the game I loved after such a bad accident one year ago.

I also took some time to imagine winning again. I visualized bombing drives off the tee and watching them land in the middle of the soft fairway. I saw myself seeing the line on the greens and watching my ball follow that line perfectly before rattling at the bottom of the cup. Hearing the roar of the crowd. Holding the trophy. Hugging my family in celebration. I imagined it all, and smiled as I daydreamed.

As per Eddie's suggestion, I finished the night by reading from a motivational book until my eyes grew heavy and I called it a night.

Wednesday morning, I took charge of my self-talk from the moment I woke up.

"I'm going to make today a great day," I whispered to myself.

As silly as it may sound, saying something so simple really did give me a kick of enthusiasm to start my day.

I continued feeding myself positive phrases all through the day.

*I am such a lucky guy.*

*I am getting better and better.*

*Good things are coming my way!*

Those were the favorites I had on mental repeat.

Did I go through my Wednesday practice round with nothing but birdies? Of course not. I hit fairways only 60-percent of the time, spent plenty of time working my way out of bunkers, and missed a few putts I should have made.

But I did *feel* better. I did make better, more consistent contact with the golf ball. My back was barely bothering me.

*I told you this stuff works,* I could imagine Eddie saying. *But it only works if you stick with it.*

And that is the key, isn't it?

Knowing what to do and actually doing it are two very different things.

Wednesday night before the tournament, I made it to the rental house early in the evening. Ashley and I swam with the kids in the heated pool, had dinner, and watched a movie the kids picked out. It was a family comedy, which was perfect for helping me stay in a feel-good state of mind.

Since my comeback had begun, this was the most positive state I had been in the night before a tournament.

Of course, *staying* positive through four ultra-competitive rounds of PGA golf would put my renewed commitment to the test.

# 26

A sport like golf requires intense focus. A lot of your thinking between shots is strategic. You and your caddie are thinking and talking about which club to use, the best approach to your next shot, how you want to handle the wind, the slopes, the hazards, and so on.

However, there are plenty of times in a competitive tournament when you're talking to yourself about what you can and can't do, often without even realizing it. As Eddie liked to remind me, your post-shot talk can get pretty negative if you're not aware of it.

After back-to-back bogeys on the ninth and 10th holes on Thursday, I caught myself muttering a familiar phrase, "Here we go again."

And at that exact moment, my lower back started bugging me. I noticed it tightening up in a way it had not done earlier in the day.

I suppose it's possible it was purely a coincidence that my back would start bothering me the moment I started getting angry at myself for the way I was playing.

Eddie wouldn't believe that.

He would be certain my mental state was affecting my

physical state. He would likely say it was my mind's way of trying to divert my inner anger, or perhaps its way of giving myself something to blame for my poor performance.

I had now experienced enough firsthand evidence of the mind-body connection Eddie preached about. I knew my mental state wasn't the reason for every single physical problem, but I was becoming convinced the mind had a lot more influence on the physical than most of us realize.

I told my brain, *I know what you're doing, and I don't need your help. My back is fine. This is about me and the mounting pressure, which I can handle. I can do this. Bring it on!*

I birdied the next hole and finished the opening round 3 strokes over par. Not my best day, but this challenging course was giving the entire field problems.

In the second round on Friday, I played better. I finished 1 over on the day, which put me 4 strokes over par for the tournament. Luckily for me, the cut line to advance to the third round was 5 over, as many players struggled during the first two rounds.

On Saturday, I woke up feeling great. I felt great before I even told myself I was going to make this day a great day. It was as though my mind was expecting to hear it. I was training it to wake up with enthusiasm and positive expectations.

With some extra pep in my step, I had one of those rounds where I was in a good rhythm from start to finish.

Oftentimes, if my long game is strong, my short game is weak, but that wasn't the case on this day. Everything was in sync.

I ended up shooting 71 on the day, 1 stroke under par. That may not sound too impressive, but it was actually the best single-round performance of my career on this difficult course.

For the tournament, I was 3 strokes over par heading into the final round on Sunday.

Most fans would not have noticed my performance on Sunday, but it marked a crucial step forward for my game.

Prior to this tournament, I had suffered too many moments where I'd let one bogey turn into another, and then a double-bogey, and then worse. I would fall apart for four or five holes in a row and never get back on track—physically or mentally. The negative chatter in my mind would get louder and louder, and soon I'd just want the tournament to end.

That didn't happen at the Memorial.

I kept feeding myself positive messages throughout the entire round.

I stayed composed when I missed a chance at a birdie and ended up with a bogey on the third hole.

*You don't have the power to change anything that happened in the past,* I told myself as I walked off the green. *But you always have the power to change what happens next. Go out there and change what happens next.*

I laughed it off when I realized my ball was covered in mud after what I thought was going to be a perfect lie on the sixth-hole fairway. I made the best contact I could and still made it onto the green with my approach shot.

On the seventh hole's monstrous 582-yard par-5, I buried my ball in the bunker to the right of the fairway after another sub-300-yard drive. But I didn't go down my usual *just-my-luck* type of self-pity thinking. I told myself this is what pro golfers deal with. This is part of the game. This is a moment to separate myself from the competition. I got back onto the fairway with my bunker shot, reached the shortgrass in front of the green with my approach shot, chipped onto the green in 4, and ended up saving par with my putt from four feet out.

After missing a five-foot putt for par on 14, I responded by sinking a twelve-foot putt for a birdie on 15.

My lower-back soreness flared up on the back nine and talking to it didn't seem to help this time, but I fought through the pain and managed to birdie two of the final four holes of the tournament.

I finished the final round with a 70, which was 1 stroke better than my previous best from the day before. I finished 1 over for the tournament.

Finishing over par is usually not a very impressive outing for a pro golfer, but at this course on this weekend, my score of 1 over was good enough for me to tie for sixteenth place. This gave me my first top-twenty finish of the season.

More importantly to me, I had gone through one of the most difficult tournaments on the Tour without losing my cool, beating myself up, or buckling to the pressure.

Sure, there wasn't as much pressure in a tournament where the world's top golfer, Scottie Scheffler, was blowing away the rest of the competition with a 10-under performance, but I was proud of how I improved just a little bit each day. I shot my personal best on this course in the third round and then beat that score in the final round.

The Memorial was the turning point I had been waiting for. A top-twenty finish and four consistent rounds of golf on one of the most difficult courses you'll ever play.

Though I didn't walk off the course with the first-place trophy I envisioned winning, I did walk off with a solid payday and a boatload of renewed confidence.

My inner doubts had been silenced.

I was back.

Or so I thought.

# 27

After the Memorial, I was feeling great. My family and I celebrated my return to top-twenty play by firing up the grill and swimming in the heated pool at the rental house. Mike and his family joined us. It was a wonderful night.

Eddie made a quick stop-by to tell me he was proud to see me playing so consistently and not getting flustered.

"How's the mental game?" he asked quietly.

"How do you think?" I smiled big. "Never better."

"I'm glad to hear it. Just remember, it's an ongoing battle. Stay on top of it. Stay disciplined. Stick to the fundamentals. Don't get lazy about them."

I told him he could count on it and I thanked him for all his help. "Once again, you saved my career."

"You're on the right track, that's for sure."

I sensed he had more to say, but he didn't want to interrupt my time with family.

The next day, Mike and I flew to Toronto and drove about an hour west to the beautiful TPC Toronto at Osprey Valley for the RBC Canadian Open. A lot of the Tour's top players would be skipping this tournament. They wanted to rest up and get ready for the following week's Major, the

U.S. Open.

I couldn't afford to take the week off. My sixteenth-place finish at the Memorial had given my career new life. Now, I needed to focus on earning enough FedExCup points to keep my Tour card for the next season. My late start to this season and my rough outings in the spring meant I had a lot of catching up to do.

On Thursday at the Canadian Open, it looked as though I would have no problem racking up some points and maybe even competing for an outright victory. I shot a 66, which was 4 under par for this par-70 course. This was my best single-round score since my return to the Tour and it was good enough to have me tied for eighth place after the first round.

My mental game was in a good place and so was my physical game. Though I wasn't wowing anybody with my power off the tee, I was finding the fairways consistently and my feel for the greens was coming back.

On Friday, I opened the second round with a bogey on the first hole, but followed that up with two-straight birdies. I didn't have another bogey the rest of the day and finished the round even better than the previous day, with a 65.

I was on fire and I couldn't help but think my improved mental game was the main reason why.

In the days leading up to the tournament, I was being kind to myself. Taking time to laugh and feel appreciative about life.

After my top-twenty performance at the Memorial, the thought of an early retirement was the last thing on my mind.

I was taking charge of my self-talk. The more I repeated positive, can-do, empowering phrases, the more natural—and believable—they felt.

*I'm feeling good and playing great,* I said to myself multiple times throughout each round as I walked up the fairway.

*I can handle this,* I said on a few different occasions after landing in the rough, the bunker, or on the far side of the green. *This is where I separate myself.*

*Things are turning my way,* I repeated throughout the day, both on and off the course.

My 5 under for the round on Friday put me at 9 under heading into the weekend, just 3 strokes behind the leader.

"You're like a changed man," Mike said to me in the locker room after the round.

"What do you mean?" I said, though I had a pretty good idea.

"In the past, missing that par on the first hole could have sent you into a tailspin, but you didn't let it bother you. You're playing like you did before ..."

He trailed off and gave me an apologetic look, worried the mere mention of my accident might trigger something negative in me.

I smiled. "I don't know that I'm quite there yet, but I'm

headed in the right direction."

Though I was 9 under after the first two rounds, I was far from the only player on fire during this tournament. It seemed like exceptionally low scores were everywhere I looked. The cut line for this tournament was 3 under, a full 8 strokes better than it was at last week's Memorial.

On Saturday, good things did indeed continue to come my way. I was in a zone like I hadn't been in well over a year. I was consistently finding the sweet spot with my drives and approach shots, and I was playing the greens better than I had all season.

I went 3 under on Saturday, putting me at 12 under for the tournament. The two leaders were sitting at 14 under, there were three players tied at 13 under, and I was tied with three others at 12 under. In other words, I was playing well, but so were a lot of other guys.

Still, I was in contention to win heading into Sunday. It had been a *long* time since I could last say that. And it felt good.

Really good.

After my Saturday round, a reporter from the Golf Channel asked me a few questions outside the clubhouse. This was the first time since my embarrassing performance at the PGA Championship that a reporter had sought me out.

"Jack, you've really turned things around these last few weeks. You're now near the top of the leaderboard heading into the final round. How are you feeling out there?"

"Thank you, yes, I'm feeling better than I have in a long, long time."

"Your back injury no longer bothering you?"

"It's a lot better than it was."

"From the outside looking in, this is a pretty dramatic turnaround from your performance at the PGA Championship. What changed for you?"

"My mental game. I've shifted my mindset. I'm focusing on what I can do instead of what I can't do. I'm trying to keep my self-talk positive and protect myself from negative messages. That's made a huge difference for me these past few weeks."

"Here you are, heading into Sunday with a chance to win. The pressure obviously goes up a notch in these situations. How do you handle that pressure and keep yourself positive?"

It was a reasonable question. Here I was, talking about the importance of my mental game, and this reporter was asking a follow-up about how I could keep my mental game sharp when the pressure turned more intense.

Yet, as soon as he asked it, I felt a slight drop in my stomach. Like an alarm bell going off to remind me that the stakes just got a whole lot higher.

I shrugged. "I just try my best to ignore the pressure and stay focused on what I can control, which is doing the best I can one shot at a time and not beating myself up when I make a mistake."

The reporter chuckled. "That sounds like good life advice, too."

"It definitely is."

"Well, I for one, am glad to see you playing so much better and I know we're all excited to watch you tomorrow."

I thanked the reporter, but as I walked away, I realized what he said was true: a *lot* of eyes would be on me tomorrow. No doubt the TV coverage would be focused on me and the comeback storyline that could draw interest from more casual fans.

This was my chance to prove to the golf world that I really was back to my pre-accident level of play. This was my chance to complete the comeback that would make headlines.

*This is your chance, Jack.*

*Please don't blow it.*

# 28

When I got back to my hotel room, I turned on the TV to watch the Golf Channel's post-round coverage of the Canadian Open. They showed a handful of my highlights and then the host and the analyst, an ex-pro, spent the next few minutes talking about the significance of my performance.

"Jack McKee has a chance to do something incredible tomorrow," the host said. "Earlier this season, watching him play, I didn't think there was any way he'd make it back to the position he is now in. If he keeps playing like he's played the last few days and actually *wins* this tournament, it will be one of the greatest comeback stories in our sport's history."

The ex-pro smiled big and shook his head. "It would be extraordinary, no question about it. This is the type of feel-good story we all need. But let me tell you, the pressure heats up in moments like this and he's going to have to keep a cool head tomorrow. It will be a great challenge. I think we'll all be pulling for him."

You would think a professional golfer in his fifteenth season as a pro would be excited to have the golf world watching his final round of a tournament. You would think

I'd be used to the pressure by now – perhaps even embracing it. I knew some players who always seemed to play their best when the pressure turned up. Unfortunately, I didn't have a long history of being one of those guys.

The pressure of this sport once overwhelmed me so badly in a tournament that I had a panic attack on the 18th green, in front of a live TV audience.

Eddie helped me overcome a lot of the anxiety and stress that once plagued me, but there were moments when nervous tension could still rattle me.

I was afraid this was going to be one of those moments.

Perhaps it was worse because I hadn't dealt with this type of pressure for so long. It had been almost two years since I was last in serious contention for a victory the night before the final round of a tournament.

Golf history is full of moments where top players went into the final round at or near the top of the leaderboard and then ended up playing their worst round of the tournament. Frankly, it happens almost every weekend.

I tried to tell myself that would not be me.

I tried to tell myself I was ready for this moment.

But I couldn't help but worry I might blow the opportunity in front of me. That I would let down Mike, my family, Eddie, and anyone else pulling for me. That I might screw up and embarrass myself in front of a national TV audience ... again.

When I went to bed that night, I tried to follow the

routine Eddie had advised. I thought about the things I was grateful for. I imagined winning the Canadian Open. I grabbed an inspirational book to feed my mind positivity before turning off the light.

But still, I tossed and turned for hours.

I reminded myself it was normal to feel nervous before such an important round of golf. The nervousness simply confirmed how important it was to me.

But the longer I struggled to fall asleep, the more that voice in my head reminded me how important sleep was and how I wasn't getting any.

As the night went on, my thoughts ran off in negative directions. Soon, I was thinking about the accident again and how angry I was that it happened.

*Why me? Why did this have to happen to me? Everything had been going great. Why am I back to grinding through the Tour, desperate to hold on to my Tour card? I thought I was past all that. I WAS past it. Then life came along and took away everything I had going for me. It isn't fair. Why can't things just be the way they were before the accident. It isn't fair!*

My thoughts were becoming more irrational and whinier the longer the night went on. I wasn't thinking clearly.

I tried everything I could think of to fall asleep.

Deep breaths. Calm visions. Telling myself to release all that anger.

But nothing calmed me down.

My mind was racing. Worries ramped up about what I

would do if I couldn't keep my Tour card beyond this season. My body was tense with nervous energy and outright anger at having to be in the desperate situation I found myself in.

All eyes were going to be on me tomorrow. Without any big expectations heading into the week, I suddenly found myself with a chance to win a tournament, and I was thinking about what all that would mean for my career. A win would not only be a big payday, but it would also give me a two-year exemption to keep playing on the PGA Tour.

In less than twenty-four hours, I could alleviate all the doubt, worry, and anger I'd been dealing with since the accident and my return to the Tour.

This was big.

This was very big.

Could I do it? Could I rise to the occasion or would I blow the opportunity?

# 29

I know what you're expecting to hear. You're probably thinking I went to the course short on rest and high on stress, and ended up playing a disastrous round from start to finish. But that's not how it happened.

Yes, after a night with barely any sleep—thinking about everything that was at stake, thinking about all the great players who fell apart in the final round, and thinking about all the people who were suddenly going to be tuning in to the Canadian Open just to see if Jack McKee could pull a Ben Hogan and come back from a bad car accident—I did walk up to the tee box on the first hole and let my nerves get the best of me. I topped my opening drive like a child trying to impress adults by how hard he could swing. My line-drive of a shot whizzed off my club and nearly took out a fan on its way to the rough on the left side of the fairway.

But it could have been a lot worse. I regrouped and actually parred the hole.

In fact, I parred the second hole too, and then racked up three birdies in a row.

Five holes into the round, I had picked up 3 strokes and was well on my way to competing for the tournament title.

On the sixth hole, I ran into my first real trouble of the day with a drive that sailed on me and landed in the far right rough. I came up short of the green on my second shot and ended up with my first bogey of the afternoon following two putts on the green.

*No big deal. Bogies happen. All you can control is what you do next,* I reminded myself.

The seventh hole was a short par-3. But I landed in the left bunker with my tee shot and ended up with another bogey.

Back-to-back bogeys.

Now, I was starting to panic.

I was starting to wonder if I had the mental toughness to handle this moment. I was questioning if I had the talent to finish the job when I needed to most. And wouldn't you know, my lower back started tightening up on me.

Every time I heard the crowd cheer in the distance, I imagined one of my competitors picking up a stroke and adding to their lead on me.

*Don't blow this, Jack. You're not going to get another opportunity like this one.*

This wasn't exactly the type of helpful self-talk I should have been feeding myself. But I couldn't help it. That negative voice in my head was taking over.

I regrouped by saving par on the eighth hole, but it was the ninth hole par-4 where my game really fell apart.

On my drive, I caught the ball with probably my best

impact of the afternoon. It hit the fairway and bounced to a total distance of 305 yards. The only problem was that it didn't stop bouncing until it landed in the bunker to the right of the fairway. From the bunker, I overshot the fairway and ended up in the rough on the *other* side, still 105 yards away from the hole. My third shot lodged the ball into the left-front ridge of the green, stopping immediately on impact. I chipped onto the green with my fourth shot. Nine feet from the hole, I misplayed the slope and missed the cup to the left. My sixth shot was an 18-inch putt for a *double*-bogey.

I knew right then I had blown this golden opportunity.

Mike tried to keep me from losing my cool as we made the turn.

"Don't even think about your score, Jack. Relax and enjoy the day, one shot at a time."

I took a deep breath. "You're right. You're absolutely right."

But after finishing the front nine 1 over par, I knew I was in big trouble.

I missed a five-foot putt for birdie on 10, then bogeyed 11 to go to 2 over on the day. After that, it was all pars and another bogey on 16 to finish the round 3 over and the tournament 9 under.

While 9 under might sound like a good score, it wasn't on this weekend when low scores were everywhere. The winner of the Canadian Open won a playoff after finishing

18 under, a full 9 strokes ahead of me. I finished the tournament tied with seven other guys in thirty-seventh place.

I've had plenty of worse rounds in my career, but what really stung about this one was not only the blown opportunity to win a tournament, which doesn't come often, but the fact that I went from 3 under after five holes to 3 *over* by the end of the round.

"*Six* strokes," I said to Mike at dinner later that evening, wincing to get comfortable in my chair as my back continued to bother me. "A six-stroke turnaround in the wrong direction. I think people would call that a meltdown."

"Nobody thinks that," Mike said. "And besides, why would you care what anyone else thinks?"

"Okay, maybe it's what *I* think. Maybe I'm the one who thinks—no, I'm the one who *knows*—I buckled to the pressure and blew my chance to win a tournament and secure my Tour card. I had it, and I blew it. I couldn't keep it together. I let my nerves get the best of me. Again."

Mike shook his head. "Guys were on fire all weekend. It was going to be a tough tourney to win even if you were flawless today."

"It's more than that. I'm telling you, from the time we walked off the course yesterday, something was different. I was worried and nervous instead of confident and feeling good. It was like I lost all my confidence overnight."

"Sounds like you might want to meet with Eddie before the U.S. Open next week. Because we both know, the pressure is only going to get bigger there."

# 30

As if he had overheard our conversation, Eddie called me later that evening.

"When are you headed to Oakmont?" he said.

"Early tomorrow."

"Great. I'm already here waiting for you. You're gonna like this place."

"What place?"

"I booked you and Mike rooms at the Oakmont Inn. Deb and I are already here."

This year's U.S. Open would be played at the historic Oakmont Country Club. Located in Oakmont, Pennsylvania, which is in the East Hills suburbs of Pittsburgh, the course was legendary. Built in 1903, Oakmont would be hosting its tenth U.S. Open.

The course was known for being one of the most difficult on the Tour, especially due to the sharp slopes on its greens. Sam Snead once famously joked that he tried to mark his ball with a coin on one of Oakmont's greens, but the coin slid off the green.

Since the accident, my strategy had been to make up for my lost distance with an impeccable short game. If my short game was going to be my advantage, this course was going to be the ultimate test.

Eddie told me he hadn't missed a U.S. Open at Oakmont since the first one he played in, back in 1983. This was one of his favorite host sites for the Open and he was not about to miss it.

Typically, Monday is the one "off" day of the week for a touring pro – assuming you played in the weekend rounds of the previous tournament. We used the day to travel, get settled into the new site, and catch up on rest. I told Eddie I planned to stay in Pittsburgh, but would stop by as soon as I got to town.

"Stop by?" he said. "Have you ever been to the Oakmont Inn?"

"No, I can't say that I have."

"It's a bed and breakfast right across the street from the club. The best place to stay. You can't beat it. I had to pull some strings, but I booked three rooms six years ago. I want you and Mike to take the other two. Trust me, you can't beat it."

It was unlike Eddie to invite me to stay with him during a PGA event week. He knew how important routine was for a professional athlete. He knew I needed to stay focused if I was going to be at my best.

"Why do I get the sense this is more of an order than an invitation?" I said.

"I *would* like to talk to you about something important,"

Eddie said. "And, to be honest with you, I think it might do your head some good to avoid locking yourself in a hotel room between rounds this week."

Eddie was onto me. He knew I had driven myself crazy with nervous internal chatter the Saturday night before the final round of the Canadian Open.

I hesitated for a moment, still not too fond of the idea of changing my original plans. But it *would* be tough to beat the location. And how could I tell Eddie no?

"I'll call you when I get there," I said.

What did I have to lose?

# 31

On Monday afternoon, Mike and I arrived in Pittsburgh, rented a car, and drove to Oakmont.

This was my first time seeing the famous course.

As we drove around it, the first thing that struck me—after the fact that the Pennsylvania Turnpike runs almost directly through the middle of it—was how there were no water hazards and virtually no trees that needed to be avoided. What the course did have plenty of were bunkers.

"One hundred and sixty-eight bunkers, to be exact," Eddie told us when we met up for dinner. "Originally a links-style course, Oakmont has some of the meanest greens you'll ever play. I think it's the toughest course in America. You won't find another pro who doesn't list it at least in his top five of toughest courses played."

"For a guy who could use some confidence right now, you're not helping," I said.

That got a laugh at the table, though I wasn't kidding.

After dinner, Eddie, Mike, and I walked the course. Several other pros and caddies were doing the same thing when we arrived. We chatted briefly with others here and there—most of them wanted to meet or pay their respects to Eddie—but everyone was pretty focused on making mental notes as they assessed the course.

A Major like the U.S. Open means something more to everyone. You could already sense some competitive tension between players, much more than you would normally feel on the Monday before a tournament.

Seeing the large, sharply sloping greens; the thick, unforgiving rough; and the famous "Church Pews" bunker located between holes three and four proved Eddie wasn't kidding about the difficulty I would be facing this week. It was clear why this course had a reputation for being so tough.

Dusk was settling over the course on this mild June evening as we strolled past the final hole. Mike was doing what caddies do in preparation for a tournament, scribbling down notes about the course. He would be advising me with those notes once the tournament was underway. Mike was a meticulous caddie who would be a great help to any pro on the Tour. I was lucky to have him on my bag.

"I'm going to head back over a few holes before we lose the sunlight," Mike said.

"Sounds good," I said. "We'll meet you back at the Inn."

Eddie and I lingered to look over the 18th green. He pointed to the empty grandstand behind us, where the luckiest fans would be seated once the tournament began.

"Let's grab a seat," he said. "Take it all in."

We took the top back row and watched the sky turn pink

and orange as the sun set over this majestic course. The beautiful, heavily treed hills of Western Pennsylvania set the scene beyond the course.

Eddie pointed to the green below us. "Can you see yourself there on Sunday, holding that trophy?"

I smiled and nodded.

"That's the one I never got," Eddie said. "Forty-nine Tour wins and seven Majors, but never the U.S. Open. I finished runner-up right here on this very course in eighty-three. I was in my early thirties and figured I would have many more opportunities to win. But I never again broke the top five in this event. I don't know what it was about the U.S. Open. I just couldn't complete the Grand Slam. And I still hear about it now and again."

Eddie was smiling, but I could tell it bothered him. The Grand Slam meant winning all four Major tournaments at least once. Only six players have ever done it. Eddie won three of the four.

"I missed it by one stroke, right down there." Eddie shook his head and chuckled. "Funny how you remember the ones that got away more than the ones you won. Shows you how powerful negative memories and emotions are."

"Come on," I said. "You're mister positive thinking. You're one of the greatest golfers of all time. Are you telling me you still live with regrets?"

"Of course, I do. Don't ever trust someone who says they have no regrets. We all do. You learn from mistakes and failures—how you respond to them makes you who you are. But no matter how necessary those setbacks may be, I've never meant anyone who enjoyed going through them. With time, you learn they were an essential part of the journey, but that doesn't mean you're glad they all happened. At least, not the ones that happened at the U.S. Open."

We both laughed, then Eddie began addressing what he really brought me here to talk about.

# 32

"How are you feeling right now?" Eddie said. "You're quieter than normal."

"I'm still not over yesterday," I said. "I blew a great opportunity to win a tournament and keep my Tour card. Those opportunities don't come along often. Especially after my accident and having to change the way I play, I know things need to set up perfectly for me to be in contention in the final round. They did, and I blew it.

"So, how do I *feel*? I'm mad as hell at myself. I'm disappointed. I'm wondering if I'll look back a few months from now, maybe years from now, and realize *that* was my chance to stay on the Tour and keep my career alive. But I blew it. How's that for a regret?"

"You weren't yourself yesterday," Eddie said. "Even on those early holes when you racked up a few birdies, I could tell something was wrong as I watched you on TV. That confidence and freedom you were playing with in the early rounds was gone. You were tight. You were overthinking. I could see it."

I sighed. "Was it that obvious?"

"To me, it was. What was going on in your head?"

"The night before, it was like I snapped back to the way I was thinking a month ago. Lots of fear. Lots of worry. I went down a path thinking how I wouldn't even be in such a desperate situation if that jackass hadn't run his car into me."

"Did you use the techniques we talked about? Seeing those emotions dissolve or float away?"

I shook my head. "I tried, but I couldn't do it. I was too angry."

Eddie nodded. "Anger—whether it's directed at yourself or someone else—makes it very difficult to eliminate negative thoughts. That's why it's so crucial to be kind to yourself first, but that takes conscious effort on your part."

"I was so worked up, I wasn't even thinking about being kind to myself. When I get like that, there's this voice inside that tells me I don't deserve to feel good. There's too much at stake and this is too serious of a situation." I paused, reflecting on what I was saying and realizing Eddie had been trying to coach me out of these exact thought patterns for the past three weeks. "I know, I know. I'm doing exactly what you taught me *not* to do."

"What do you think caused this shift back to some of your old ways of thinking?"

"The pressure," I said. "I kept thinking of everything that was at stake. How I was so close to the lead and playing so well. How a victory would keep me on the Tour. All those things.

"At first, I was excited about what was in front of me. Then my excitement turned to worry. I thought about what a disappointment it would be if I couldn't come through. I started thinking more about what I had to lose instead of just playing free. I started fearing what would happen if I had a meltdown. My worries turned to full-on panic."

Eddie nodded. "I assumed it was something like that. You're obviously not out of the woods yet with the mental shift you need to make. You suffered a traumatic setback last year. It took you to a dark place mentally. That dark place, as unpleasant as it is, started to feel more natural for you. You're now working your way out of it, but you're reverting back to it as soon as the pressure turns up. There's still a good portion of your mind weighed down with fear, worry, and anger. It's only going to get worse as this season goes on if you don't put a stop to it."

"I just can't seem to do it. When the pressure turns up like it did Saturday night, negative thoughts bombard me. I start thinking about how lucky I was on certain shots and how that luck is bound to run out. I start worrying about my back pain flaring up; what will I do then? I start fearing what people will say if I fall apart and embarrass myself. In no time, I'm thinking of worst-case scenarios months down the road. Losing my Tour card, telling Ashley and the kids we have to move, never playing pro golf again. It's like I can't help myself."

"The war within your mind never ends," Eddie said.

"It's a constant battle.

"When things go wrong in life, especially those big catastrophes you didn't see coming, it leads to all the negative emotions we've talked about. But it also makes you more prone to panic. You worry about never getting back what you once had. You overthink every new decision you have to make. You overreact to every new setback that comes up.

"Panic makes you expect the worst possible outcome. Our tendency to panic might have helped our ancestors avoid the more common life-or-death threats they had to deal with, but it rarely benefits us in our modern everyday lives.

"Once you start panicking, you become irrational. And when you become irrational, you become agitated, anxious, and angrier. Those emotions make you even more irrational. It's a vicious, self-fulfilling cycle and it's tough to get out of.

"But there is a solution. It's a very simple-sounding solution, but if you can be disciplined enough to embrace it, you'll save yourself from a lot of worry, stress, and panic in life."

# 33

Panic was something I had struggled with all my life.

Since I was a kid, I had a bad habit of fearing whatever problem I was dealing with was going to be permanent and would never get better. Eddie had been helping me overcome this type of thinking for the past three years, but it was easy for me to fall back into it—especially after the accident that derailed my career and made me question everything Eddie had taught me.

"I'm willing to try whatever you think can help me stay on track," I said. "I'm tired of being so up and down mentally. I'm tired of going down a dark path whenever things don't go my way."

Eddie gave me a fatherly pat on the back. "Don't be so hard on yourself. We *all* deal with this stuff. It isn't easy to stay in a positive mental state when there is so much adversity to deal with. And what you've been through *was* traumatic. Give yourself a break.

"But here's something you need to understand. I believe the biggest cause of stress is worry. Worry leads to stress, which leads to panic. So, you must make eliminating worry a priority. **The best way to eliminate worry is to tell**

**yourself: You are not allowed to worry about anything beyond this day, this twenty-four-hour period. You have to take life *one* day at a time. Don't worry about any of tomorrow's *potential* problems today."**

"That's it? Take life one day at a time? That's your solution?"

Eddie chuckled. "I know it sounds obvious, but **when I got serious about studying successful people, I noticed that I never encountered a truly successful person who worried much at all. We know how bad worry is for our health, but I'm also convinced worry blocks us from success."**

"But we *have* to think about the future. We have to plan for things beyond this day. It would be irresponsible not to."

"Of course, but planning is different from worrying. Planning is solution-focused. It focuses on preparing for problems, but then finding a solution and delivering a positive outcome. Worrying, on the other hand, is problem-focused. It envisions a problem coming to fruition and then replays that negative outcome again and again in our minds. Nothing good comes from worrying. It is fear-based thinking.

"Of course, nobody *wants* to worry. When you tell someone to stop worrying, it doesn't do much good. Everyone wishes they *could* stop worrying.

"The solution is to tell yourself not to worry about

anything beyond *today*. **Ninety-nine-percent of the things most of us worry about are things beyond this day. If you refuse to allow yourself to worry about anything beyond today, you've eliminated almost all your worries.**

"If you tell your mind to never worry again, it will resist that command. Worrying is such a way of thinking for most of us that it seems unrealistic to never do it again. But if you tell your mind to stop worrying about anything beyond this day, it can accept that. That seems like a reasonable tradeoff. That seems doable. It's a lot easier to stop worrying when you tell your mind it can still worry, but just not about anything beyond what it can do something about today."

"At that point, aren't you just delaying the worry, putting it off until tomorrow instead of dealing with it now?" I said, thinking I had pointed out a flaw in Eddie's logic.

"Have you ever noticed how dealing with a crisis in the moment is never as bad as you worried it would be? Most of us can respond just fine to whatever trouble we're dealing with in the moment. We can attack and adapt to obstacles as they come. Sure, you might have to deal with disappointment or grief over something, which is not enjoyable, but it has been my experience that ruminating about how bad something might end up being is almost always worse than the actual dealing with it when it happens. And most of the time, our worries never end up happening at all, which makes worrying about the future even more pointless.

"We drive ourselves crazy when we get lost in worries about the future, fears about how bad future scenarios *might* be. **You can't be your best today, right now, if you're worried about tomorrow.** We lose our focus on what needs to be done right now when we allow ourselves to focus on fears of the future.

"Avoid worrying about things that *can't* be done today. At the end of the night, when you've completed all the tasks and plans you can, it's pointless to worry about anything you have to do tomorrow. When tomorrow comes, *that's* when you can deal with it.

"You have to compartmentalize your thinking. **When your mind starts racing with worries, ask yourself if there is anything you can do about those things *right this moment.* If the answer is no, then tell yourself you are not allowed to worry about it. Limit the time period you are allowing yourself to worry about. Limit it to today and today only.**

"If you think of a task you forgot to complete today, then by all means write it down and schedule it for tomorrow, but stop thinking about it if the moment to work on it has already passed.

"This little rule to live one day at a time has saved me and countless others from so much worry and stress. The fact is, we can do nothing about yesterday and none of us really knows what tomorrow will bring until tomorrow gets here. We can deal with whatever happens then.

"I believe God gives us the strength and power to deal with one day at a time. Nothing more and nothing less. **You have to start each day fresh, no matter what happened yesterday. And you can't do anything about tomorrow until tomorrow actually gets here, so it makes no sense to dwell on various negative scenarios playing out.**"

"What about visualization?" I said. "You taught me to imagine myself going through negative situations so I would be better prepared for them."

Eddie nodded. "The difference is the outcome you are imagining. I've always said you need to visualize *positive* outcomes. Worries focus on negative outcomes. They focus on all the ways you might fail. They focus on all the reasons a bad situation is bound to get worse.

"Instead, you should be visualizing positive outcomes. That means seeing yourself recover brilliantly from a bad shot. It means imagining all the things that could go right for your career instead of all that could go wrong. It means expecting a bad situation to turn around in your favor. That's how you train your mind to succeed.

"On Saturday night, when you were worrying about all the things that could go wrong, were you seeing yourself overcoming those problems or were you focusing on the problem itself and feeling the feelings that a negative outcome would bring?"

"The latter," I said.

"That's what worries do. They keep your focus on

problems, not solutions.

**"It's helpful to prepare for problems and visualize overcoming them. It's stressful to think about those same problems and let them play out with negative outcomes again and again. That's the difference between positive visualization and negative worry.**

"I'm sure when you were recovering from your accident, you had many nights where you wondered if you would ever be the same golfer again. I'm guessing you worried about whether your career was over and wondered what you would do with the rest of your life. Maybe you worried about your finances with all the hospital bills and how you would keep earning if you couldn't play golf anymore. Maybe you worried about whether the pain you were feeling would ever go away. Am I right?"

My stomach got uneasy just thinking of those worries again. I had stewed about them for months.

"Yes," I said, "you're right."

"Ruminating about each of those worries was conditioning your mind to seek out negative outcomes. The more you thought about them, the more your subconscious accepted them as your fate.

"Notice how all those worries were focused on negative outcomes occurring well into the future.

"The thing is, **when we remind ourselves to take life one day at a time, we tend to be pretty optimistic about whatever we're dealing with right this moment, this day.**

**We feel in control. We feel good about our ability to handle it. It's when we go down those dark roads too far into the future where we feel less and less in control.**

"We can only control the present moment. Our effort and our attitude in the present moment is always under our control. And we feel good when we're in control. But as soon as you go too far beyond this present moment, that's where you can feel overwhelmed by your lack of control.

"The solution is simple. When worries try to take over your mind, remember to live one day at a time. Stay in this day, *this* moment."

The sun had set and the stars were brightening. I took a deep breath, inhaling the nighttime air and thinking about what Eddie was saying.

"Eddie, you have a way of taking the simplest ideas and making them sound like the most brilliant, life-changing advice I've ever heard."

We both laughed.

"The simplest solutions *are* usually the most effective," Eddie said.

# 34

Eddie's rule to live one day at a time and to recognize how most negative thoughts were focused on things that happened in the past or things that *might* happen in the future may have been obvious, but it was something most of us rarely think about. Especially me.

How often had I let my mind get consumed by past mistakes or worries about what might go wrong next week or ten years from now? How much time had I wasted every day with such negative thoughts? How much extra stress had I created for myself by replaying past mistakes or imagining bad events in the future that never came about?

On our walk back to the Inn, Eddie reminded me that this one-day-at-a-time philosophy also applied to golf in a very important way.

"The more you can compartmentalize your golf game, the better you will play," he said. "That means more than making sure you aren't worrying about tomorrow's round today. It means focusing only on this round, this hole, this single shot. That's where all your power is. In this present moment."

I spent Tuesday and Wednesday training in the morning

and practicing all day. I made it a point to notice whenever I had an anxiety-producing thought. As soon as I did—as soon as I felt that little drop in my stomach signaling nervousness, fear, or worry—I asked myself, is this something I can do anything about today?

Eddie was right. Almost every time, the thought was focused on some fear about what might happen days or weeks from now. Or it would be the pain of regret or resentment about something in the past. Either way, it violated Eddie's rule to take life one day at a time.

When I caught myself thinking such thoughts, I would tell myself, *Focus on the present. If that day comes, I will be able to handle it then.*

What if I lose my Tour card? What will I do with my life? How will I earn my living? Will we lose our house?

*If that day comes, I will be able to handle it then.*

I'm at the age where players usually start dealing with more injuries. Will the injuries from my accident make me more prone to future injuries?

*If that day comes, I will be able to handle it then.*

What if I don't make the cut this weekend? Will that prove Major events are just too much pressure for me?

*If that happens, I will be able to handle it then.*

This simple reminder made me feel calmer and more in control of everything I worried about. It also kept me focused on the here and now as I practiced. One hole, one swing at a time.

What if my back starts bothering me on the back nine? *I will be able to handle it then.*

Oakmont is one of the toughest courses in the world and I've never played it before; will I be at a disadvantage once the tournament starts? *I will take it one hole at a time, just like everyone else.*

These bunkers are everywhere. I hope I'm ready for them. *What can I do about it today? Spend extra practice time working out of the sand. Take some time to visualize how I will get out of those bunkers.*

Asking myself what I can do about a situation today helped me clarify what I did or did not have control of.

Mentally, I was back on track after my poor performance in the final round of the Canadian Open. Eddie had saved me again.

# 35

I was nervous but excited early Thursday morning as I walked out of the Oakmont Inn. I was on my way to hit some practice balls before the first round of the U.S. Open. Just as I stepped out the front door, I heard Eddie's voice.

"It's a beautiful day to play the greatest game God ever invented," he said.

He and Debbie were sitting at a small table in front of the Inn, sipping coffee. She gave me a warm smile and he raised his mug at me.

"That it is," I said with a return smile, acknowledging the bright, sunny morning. "Warm and sunny, highs in the eighties, sure beats working for a living."

Eddie chuckled as he stood up. He walked over to me, gave me a firm handshake with his right hand, and squeezed my shoulder with his left.

"I'm not going to annoy you with advice all weekend," he said. "But if you need anything at all, just ask. You know where to find me."

"Thank you, Eddie, I appreciate it."

"This is your day. Have fun and enjoy it. There's no place like Oakmont."

"One shot at a time," I said.

"You got it."

As I walked away, I was hit with the sudden realization that Eddie had calmed my nerves considerably with his short morning greeting.

In an instant, he had shifted my perspective from being nervous about how I would hold up playing one of golf's most difficult courses to feeling excited that I was *getting* to play on this legendary course.

That's the thing about the great competitors. For all of Eddie's talk about this being the most difficult course he ever played, it was also his favorite. He loved it. He wished he was getting to play it today.

**The great ones never run from the challenges of life. They embrace them. They enjoy them. They get better because of them.**

How's that for reframing? How's that for a mental shift?

# 36

One hundred and fifty-six golfers were competing at this year's U.S. Open. Only ten were under par after the first round. That's how difficult this course was playing.

Luckily for me, I was one of those ten players.

Mike and I had talked all week about how my short game would be key. Not only putting, but I would need to make sure I was flushing my irons. So much of your performance on the greens at a place like Oakmont depended on where you landed on the green.

We also talked about not getting rattled. Bunkers and bogeys were going to be part of playing this course. We were under no delusions that I might somehow avoid every sand trap and make every putt. We decided in advance I would need to keep reminding myself that how I *responded* to this course's obstacles would be the difference-maker.

And that's pretty much how my first round went.

I played even-par golf on the first five holes, then bogeyed the sixth. But I responded with back-to-back birdies on seven and eight. On the back nine, I followed a similar path. I bogeyed 15, but then finished the round with a birdie on 18.

I was 1 under par for the day, joining just nine other players who finished the first round below par. While I wasn't about to bust out the champagne, I was proud of how I played. I stayed focused on one shot at a time and responded well mentally to my bogeys. I didn't get flustered.

All through the round, I focused on feeding my mind positive self-talk and focusing on one hole, one shot at a time.

"Next shot," Mike said immediately when we watched my tee shot land in the left side bunker on 15.

I gave him a nod, knowing exactly what he meant. There was no reason to get upset about landing in the sand. We knew this would be part of playing this course. My focus had to be on the *next* shot, regardless of what happened on the previous shot.

That night, after some post-round practice work, Mike and I had dinner with Eddie and Debbie. We shared a lot of laughs and barely talked about my first-round performance. The table knew I needed to give my mind a break from thinking about the course and just focus on laughing and feeling good.

Of course, it's a lot easier to feel good about yourself when you're in the top ten at a Major.

I opened my Friday round with a drive into the right side rough, followed by an approach shot that landed in the rough again, followed by overshooting the green. I ended up with a bogey on the opening hole par-4.

That ended up being my one and only bogey of the day.

It was incredible.

On a course where most of the world's top players were struggling to stay under par, I was landing in all the right places after that opening hole. I was also lucky to finish my round early on Friday. Winds picked up and the rain rolled through later in the afternoon, making a difficult course even tougher for everyone battling through the conditions. Play was eventually halted late in the day

After my initial bogey, I racked up two birdies and finished the round 1 under. That score put me at 2 under for the tournament.

This course was playing so difficult that my score of 2 under was good enough to put me in a tie for second place.

The guy who four weeks ago shot two of the worst rounds you'll ever see at a Major tournament was now headed into the weekend tied for second at the U.S. Open. Never before in my career was I ranked this high at a Major after two rounds. And I was doing it on one of the toughest courses in America. I couldn't believe it was happening.

Neither could many members of the media.

# 37

"What's been the key to your sudden turnaround these last four weeks?" a reporter asked me in the media tent after my second-round performance.

"Shifting my mindset and eliminating negative self-talk," I said, being as honest as I could. "Eddie Collins has been helping me get my mental game back on track these last few weeks. He also told me how difficult this course would be. I think that helped me handle it much better. **When you expect things to be difficult, it's a lot easier to overcome those difficulties when you encounter them.**"

"How are you feeling physically?" another reporter asked.

"The best I've been all year. It's incredible how much the physical follows the mental. I used to think that type of stuff was silly. I'm a believer now."

To be clear, I wasn't feeling 100-percent physically. My back was sore, especially by the end of eighteen holes, and I still couldn't hit the ball as far as I could prior to my accident. But I was feeling the best I had felt since my return to the Tour. My knee was fine and I was managing my back the best I could with my training routine and self-talk. It seemed to be working.

I'm sure landing enough putts to sit near the top of the leaderboard was also doing wonders for how good I was feeling.

"How do you plan to handle the pressure of being near the top heading into the weekend?" a reporter asked.

I smiled. "One shot at a time."

# 38

Friday evening, I watched dark clouds and rain roll through Oakmont Country Club from my room at the Inn. Watching a summer thunderstorm from the window of my bedroom made me feel like a kid again. It eased my mind, giving me something to think about other than golf.

However, when it was time to call it a night, I started hearing those pesky thoughts of self-doubt once again.

*Can you keep this up? How many times have you been in situations like this and blown it?*

*The weather this weekend is going to make this course even harder. You need a new strategy. What worked so far probably won't work from here on out.*

*You sure caught some lucky breaks today. Getting your round in early gave you an advantage over guys you have no business being in front of. After all that good luck, you're due for some bad, don't you think?*

I remembered Eddie's advice and asked myself as I lay in bed, *Am I worrying about something beyond this day?*

Yes.

*Is there anything I can do about it right now?*

No!

*Then don't allow yourself to think about anything negative beyond this day. If things go south tomorrow, you'll handle it when it happens. You will attack and adapt. Just as you have so far in this tournament.*

This inner dialogue worked. It was as though I mentally shut the door on anything negative beyond this current twenty-four-hour period.

I took some time to envision myself making the perfect bunker shot to get back on the green. I saw myself chipping onto the green and watching my ball spin backwards toward the hole, coming to a stop just a couple of inches away from the cup. I saw myself driving the ball, feeling perfect sweet-spot contact, hearing that *ping*, and watching the ball land safely in the middle of the fairway.

*There is no reason to worry about tomorrow,* I told myself. *The power is in the present. Whatever comes your way tomorrow you will deal with then. And you will deal with it calmly and successfully.*

*Good things are coming my way.*

I drifted off into a peaceful sleep as the rain pattered against my window and the wind howled through the Western Pennsylvania night.

# 39

Why is it that so often in life, just when everything is going great, something comes along and knocks you off track? You get completely blindsided by a setback you thought you had moved past.

It happened to me when a guy drove his car into my leg. And it happened to me in the third round of the U.S. Open.

Though my setback on the golf course was obviously not quite so dramatic, it still caused fears and doubts to rush back to the forefront of my mind.

Through most of the round, I didn't play horribly on Saturday. But I also didn't play as well as several other players in the field.

The soaking from the previous night's storm had slowed down the greens for everyone and drives off the tee weren't rolling as far as they had been. For a player like me, whose distance off the tee had been an issue ever since my accident, those bounces and rolls had really helped me gain some yardage in the early rounds.

Twelve of the remaining sixty-seven players who made the weekend cut shot rounds under par on Saturday.

This time, I was *not* one of them.

On the third hole, I landed in the famous "Church Pews" bunker to the left of the fairway. This is probably the most famous bunker in all of golf. It's thirteen rows of tall, dense grass surrounded by tons of sand (more than 550 tons of sand, to be exact). The treacherous bunker stretches 102 yards long and 42 yards wide. You can't *not* see it when you step up to the third-hole tee box. Eddie always told me we have a tendency to end up wherever we focus. That's exactly what happened to me on the third hole. Luckily, I landed in the sand of the bunker and not the tall grass. I ended up with a bogey.

On the fourth hole, I landed right back in those Church Pews, (holes three and four wrapped around the giant bunker). I finished with another bogey.

"How can a guy hit the exact same bunker twice in a row?" I imagined viewers asking. "I guess Jack McKee found a way."

"Next shot," Mike reminded me, shaking me out of the imaginary comments in my head.

I parred the next several holes, but I left a putt one inch short on the ninth, which would have given me my first birdie of the day.

On the back nine, it was hole number 12 where adversity blindsided me.

The longest hole on the course that day, at 617 yards, I had it in my head I needed to make up ground.

That's what Oakmont does to you. Every hole is so

tough; it feels like there are so few opportunities to catch up once you fall behind.

I knew lower scores were being posted by everyone around me and I was falling behind. I feared my below-average distance on drives was a major reason why. I wasn't getting the help of long rolls anymore. I needed to make up for it.

On my tee shot, I swung hard, trying to kill the ball. On my follow-through, I felt a sharp pain in my lower back and let out an audible "Ah." My ball ended up hitting a bunker left of the fairway.

"You okay, Jack?" Mike said, placing a hand on my shoulder.

"I'm not sure." I took a moment to let the sharp pain subside, hoping my lower back wouldn't lock up on me, as it had sometimes done during my rehabbing last year.

I handed Mike my driver and leaned over to stretch out my lower back as best I could. I had been feeling so much better over the last few weeks, I thought the worst of my back issues were behind me. I was now being taught by Old Man Adversity just how wrong I was.

Mike's concerned eyes were fixed on me, waiting for me to confirm whether I was okay. It seemed like all the fans in our vicinity had the same concerned look on their faces.

"I think I'm alright," I said, exhaling with relief that my back didn't start cramping up. "I just need to walk it off and keep moving."

I took a few cautious steps forward and then picked up steam as we walked to my bunker-buried ball. The way it landed, I had to chip my way onto the fairway. From there, I was still more than 360 yards away from the hole. My goal was to lay up with my 3-iron and get to about 120 yards of the pin. I had no choice but to put my back to the test with a nice, hard swing.

I took a few practice swings, wincing each time and staying cautious about following through too hard. But each swing did feel a little better as my back got used to the motion. ("Motion is lotion," my physical therapist used to say.)

*I know what you're doing,* I said to my brain. *You're trying to distract me from the pressure of this tournament. I don't need you to do that. I am fine. I can handle it. With each swing, I'm feeling better.*

As crazy as it may sound, that self-talk did help alleviate the pain. It wasn't all gone, but it was better.

Still, the pain was enough to alter my swing slightly. I ended up with an ugly shot that landed in the right side rough, 140 yards from the pin.

With my fourth shot, I landed on the green, but 50 feet from the pin on this par-5. I couldn't afford another bogey. On my putt, I went hard for the cup – much *too* hard – and watched my ball roll past the target, catch a slope in the wrong direction, and finally stop twelve feet on the other side of the green. So much for avoiding a bogey.

I left my bogey putt an inch to the right of the cup and I

ended up with a *double* bogey on the hole. My first of the tournament.

Sitting at 4 over on the day, this was a gut-check moment for me. Would I keep it together or let fear and doubt overtake me?

What would Eddie say?

He would remind me it's my choice. *I* get to choose how I respond to this moment.

I chose to take control of my self-talk.

*My back will loosen up with each swing. The worst is behind me. I can handle this. I will finish strong.*

This was much different from the way I normally talked to myself after a double-bogey.

I birdied 14 and 15, then parred the next two holes.

On the 18th and final hole of the day, I landed in the right-side rough off the tee. It wasn't the worst spot to be in. But on my approach shot, I didn't quite clear the bunker on the right front edge of the green. My bunker shot got me back on the green, but my ball stopped in its tracks almost as soon as it landed. From 15-feet out, I again misjudged the speed of the greens and failed to put enough power behind my putt. It came to a stop two inches short and I tapped in for another bogey.

I finished 3 over par for the day and was now 1 over for the tournament. It had been such a difficult tournament that despite dropping 3 strokes in round three, I had only fallen to sixth place.

But that still left me 5 strokes behind the leader, my old rival Owen Carmichael III, who was leading the field at 4 under.

Just when it seemed like I was catching all the breaks and things were going my way, life had thrown me another curve ball. My back, which had been improving so much over the past month, now felt tender with each step and every swing.

On the eve of the final round of the U.S. Open, after dropping from 1 stroke behind the leader to 5 strokes behind, I knew if there was anyone who could help me avoid a final-round meltdown it was Eddie Collins.

# 40

After the third round, I spent an hour doing the exercises and stretching techniques I learned from my physical therapist. I then went through the process of applying ice followed by heat to my lower back. I knew I needed to rest my back as much as possible before Sunday's final round. I also knew I needed to keep my mental game sharp. I couldn't allow myself to have another worry-filled night like I did before the final round of the Canadian Open.

When I knocked on Eddie's door, he welcomed me in and invited me to join him on the balcony outside his second-story room.

"I see who got the primo suite," I said with a smile as I walked onto the balcony, taking a deep breath of fresh air before sitting down cautiously in one of the two chairs next to the small table. "I'm not taking Debbie's seat, am I?"

He shook his head. "She went to dinner with some friends. I told her I had a hunch I'd be busy tonight."

"You know me well," I said. "Any last-minute advice for how I can stay in this thing? I'm not under the delusion that I can make up five strokes, but a top-ten finish would earn me a chunk of the points I need to keep my card."

"Jack, you can still win this thing."

I chuckled. "I appreciate your optimism."

"You've done it before. Three years ago, at the Gateway. Your first PGA win."

"That was a little different," I said. "That wasn't a Major, where all the top players in the world are at their best. And it wasn't on a course where it takes a minor miracle just to break even in a round."

"It happens. Paul Lawrie came back from ten strokes down to win the British Open in ninety-nine. Arnie came back from seven strokes behind to win the U.S. Open in 1960. Just a few years ago, Justin Thomas won the PGA Championship after being down seven strokes."

"But those comebacks weren't on a course like Oakmont."

Eddie huffed. "You don't know your golf history. Johnny Miller was down six strokes heading into the final round at the seventy-three U.S. Open right here at Oakmont. He shot a sixty-three on his final round and won."

"Wow," I said, genuinely impressed that a guy could score so low on a course like this.

"Got any more excuses for me?"

"Did you see what happened to me on twelve?"

"I did. Looked like you were in some pain. But you shook it off. You finished strong. How's your back feeling now?"

"Tender. I'm worried about it. I feel like it's another one

of those moments where life is slapping me in the face just when things were turning for the better. Why does it seem like this *always* happens to me?"

Eddie was silent for a moment. His jaw was clenched. He looked like he was thinking carefully about what he wanted to say next, like he didn't want to say something he would regret.

"Jack, can I tell you something that might hurt your feelings?"

I raised my eyebrows, surprised at what Eddie was getting at. "Fire away."

"You whine too much. And it's keeping you from being the best you can be."

# 41

To have my childhood hero tell me I whine too much felt like a punch to the gut. For about ten seconds, I fought the urge to defend myself. I wanted to tell him I was just being honest, and that he didn't know what it was like to go through what I had been through.

But then, I realized he was right.

I slumped back in my chair, as though I was conceding.

"I don't want you to feel bad about yourself," he said. "But if you don't stop with always looking for excuses, always looking for things to be upset about, always looking for ways you got dealt a bad hand; you're going to end your career early and live a bitter life.

"Jack, I've told you this before. What you go looking for, you will find. Yes, life will throw obstacles your way. It always has and it always will. Some are going to be worse than others. But it's how you *respond* to those obstacles that determine where you end up. If all you do is complain about them or see yourself as a victim to them, you're going to be miserable.

"Yes, life is hard. Yes, the game of golf is hard. But it's also a lot of fun! **Life throws you new obstacles all the**

**time. But it also throws you new opportunities! The key is what you choose to focus on.**

"I just watched you go toe-to-toe with the best golfers in the world on the hardest course in America for three days. And here you are in sixth place. This is one year after an accident that would have ended most people's careers. It's only a month after you were playing the worst golf of your life. And yet, all you're thinking about is how your back started hurting again and how life is being unfair to you.

"Here's the truth. Life is unfair. Nobody ever said it wasn't. Yes, you have a bad back. But guess what? Every other player out there has a bad something they're dealing with.

"**Until you start focusing on what you have and what you can do—instead of what you don't have and what you can't do—you're going to keep creating the same problems for yourself over and over again.**

"At some point, you have to change the way you think and stick with it! I'm not always going to be here to talk you off the ledge."

I had never seen Eddie this fired up before. He was fed up with my constant negative thinking and he was calling me out on it.

Rightly so.

"You've got the opportunity of a lifetime right in front of you," he said. "What I wouldn't give to be in your shoes right now, with one more round at the U.S. Open just five shots off the lead. I can't let you throw this opportunity away. I can't let you sabotage yourself with negative thinking."

My eyes lowered. I stared blankly at the balcony floor.

It was silent between us for what was probably only thirty seconds, but felt like ten minutes. Eddie was waiting for me to respond.

"You're right," I finally said. "I know I need to change the way I think and I haven't done it. I keep slipping back to the same old scripts about all my bad breaks, but I've got so much to be thankful for. I've got a family who loves me and, at least for the rest of this season, a career doing something I really do love. I don't know what my problem is."

"I do," Eddie said. "You haven't completed the mental shift you need to complete. There is one more step that just might complete this shift for you. And I believe it will help you play the best round of golf you're capable of playing tomorrow."

I looked up and saw my mental coach grinning. The kick in the pants I needed was over; he had said his piece and it knocked me out of my self-involved thinking.

He showed me what I was doing wrong. Now it was time to tell me how to fix it.

# 42

The sky was now dark and the air was cooling down. Eddie went inside and came back with drinks. What he said was "Pennsylvania's finest cold lager" for him and an ice water for me. (I had downed a few ibuprofen tablets for my sore back and didn't want to mix them with anything stronger than water.)

"I hope I wasn't too harsh with you before," he said. "I know you've been through hell this past year."

I shook my head after taking a refreshing sip. "I needed a kick in the butt. You're absolutely right. When I complain like that, I'm doing the exact thing you've told me not to do. It keeps me stuck in a negative state."

Eddie nodded and smiled, pleased he was finally getting through to me.

"I want you to know how proud I am of the progress you've made so far," he said. "It may not always seem like it, but you have made a significant shift in your thinking over the last few weeks. You are thinking and playing much better than you were a month ago."

"That's for sure," I said.

"I want you to remember this process we've been

talking about the next time you get hit by some major setback. Look at what you've learned to do and repeat these steps.

"First, be kind to yourself. Life is hard and bad things are going to happen through no fault of your own. When they do, don't hold on to anger or resentment and don't beat yourself up. Know it's simply a part of life, no matter how hard you've been working or how positive you've been thinking. **Be good to yourself. Lighten up and laugh at life. Then, take charge of how you respond to adversity. It's your response that makes the difference.**

"Once you've lightened up and let go of your anger, you can think clearly about how you need to respond. And the nonnegotiable for responding to any adversity is to **completely eliminate any thought of quitting. Thinking about giving up will only delay your ability to get back on track and do the things you need to do.** It's fine to give yourself a deadline; something like, if this doesn't work out within the next twelve months, I will decide on a new goal. But until that deadline is met, don't even think about quitting on your current goal. Don't give your subconscious any opposing goal that might hold you back. Life's a game, but it's a very challenging game. You can win the game only if you keep playing it and only if you refuse to quit.

"Once you've established that quitting is not an option, then it's time to get back to the fundamentals of winning the war within your mind. That means feeding your mind positive things and protecting it from negative things. You've got to be ruthless about this. **You've got to feed yourself positive media and positive self-talk. You've got to be grateful every day and visualize the things you want to see happen. You've also got to protect your mind from all the negative noise out there.** The vast majority of messages the average person is exposed to each day are negative. You've got to be aware of this and protect yourself as much as you can.

"Next, you've got to win the war against worry by taking life one day at a time. Plan and prepare for what you want to see happen, but **don't allow yourself to worry about anything beyond the day you're currently living in**. If something bad happens tomorrow, you'll be able to handle it then. When a worry pops up, ask yourself if there is anything you can possibly do about it today, right now. If the answer is no, tell yourself you are not allowed to think about it anymore. Establish a rule that says you won't allow yourself to worry about anything beyond this day. And have the discipline to follow that rule. Don't dwell on things you can't control right this moment. For golf, this means taking things one round, one hole, and one shot at a time. Don't look back and don't look too far ahead. The next shot is always the most important shot.

"And that brings us to one final mental technique you need to embrace if you want to fully make the shift from dark to light, from helpless to hopeful. This step can only be taken once you've taken the others. Otherwise, you won't be able to believe it. You'll question yourself too much.

"Jack, I think you're ready for the final step. It's the most important thing you need to do as you prepare for tomorrow's final round."

# 43

"I'll warn you in advance," Eddie said, "this final step is simple. Some might even call it silly, but it works."

"You've got an amazing ability to build anticipation," I said with a smile.

"Here goes. **You must *act as if something really great is about to happen.* Choose to believe something really big is coming your way. Choose to believe a miracle is just about to happen in your life. Choose to believe your greatest success is inevitable as long as you keep moving forward.**

"The cynics out there will tell you it's dangerous to get your hopes up. They'll say you are only setting yourself up to be disappointed. They'll tell you it's irresponsible and you need to tamp down your expectations. Don't believe them. In golf or any other profession, all the great achievers I've ever known or studied had what most people would call *unreasonably* high expectations for what they could achieve. Then, they would go out and live up to those expectations. As I've told you before, **life has an uncanny tendency to follow your expectations**."

I nodded politely, but lowered my eyes. Eddie picked

up on my skeptical vibes.

"I know it's hard to buy into this after everything you've been through," he said. "You weren't *expecting* life to throw you the trouble it did. I'm not suggesting you can prevent all negative things by only expecting good things. That's not how life works and you will set yourself up for some unpleasant surprises if you think it does. But you can *and must* expect to overcome any negative thing that comes your way. You *can* expect to rise above the difficulties you will surely face.

"I know what you've been through has raised serious doubts in your mind about whether you're capable of achieving your career goals. I know it has made you doubt everything I taught you in the past. But if these last few weeks have taught you anything, haven't they taught you the importance of believing in yourself again? Haven't they proved how important it is to be hopeful and optimistic?

"I'm asking you to take the next step and ***act as if*** **something really great is about to happen. Dare to get your hopes up. Dare to expect *great* things to come your way."**

"I'm not gonna lie to you, Eddie. I am worried about getting my hopes too high and suffering through another major disappointment."

"It's a risk you have to take. **If you want something great to happen, you've got to start believing it will. You've got to start *acting* as if it's about to.**

"**When you start acting as if something great is about**

**to happen, you don't dread what tomorrow might bring, you get excited about what lies ahead. You don't wallow in self-pity about how good things used to be, you get fired up about what's next. You don't agonize over a mistake or a bad tee shot, you embrace the opportunity to turn it around and make something great out of it.**

"Acting as if something great is about to happen is the ultimate hopeful attitude. And I'm telling you, **I can't explain exactly why this happens, but when you start acting like something great is about to happen, great things *do* start happening.**"

"And what happens when something great doesn't happen?" I said. "What happens when I get my hopes up, thinking I'm going to make the big shot or win the big trophy, and then I don't? Because you and I both know you can't win every tournament you play in."

"The reason for acting as if something great is about to happen is not an attempt at magic. It doesn't guarantee victory. Nothing can do that. But, **acting as if something great is about to happen will put you in the ideal mental and physical state to make your future success most likely to happen.** It will ensure you are at your best.

"Remember the parking brake analogy? How certain emotions will hold you back from being your best?"

"Sure."

"Well, self-doubt is one of those destructive emotions. **Self-doubt prevents you from being your best. You have**

**to eliminate it. Nothing will hold back your performance as much as your own self-doubt.**

"All great athletes and achievers have learned to quiet the voice of self-doubt and believe in themselves. It's the only way to reach your full potential. **The best way I've found to eliminate self-doubt and raise your expectations is to constantly be telling yourself, 'Something really great is about to happen.' And then *act as if* it truly is about to happen.** *Act as if* you have the power to make that something great happen.

"When you say that to yourself, notice how it feels. Notice how much anxiety evaporates. Notice how you stand taller and feel lighter. Notice how you want to smile. Notice the excitement that bubbles up inside. Notice how you feel stronger and more in control of your life.

"'Something really great is *about* to happen.' Repeat that over and over. At night before you fall asleep. First thing in the morning. All through the day. Repeat it over and over again until it becomes a natural part of your thinking.

"That's how you build hope. That's how you raise your expectations. **I can't guarantee you'll always win if you adopt this attitude, but I can guarantee you'll have a much better chance to win if you do.**

"If you went through the day truly expecting something really great was just about to happen, how would you carry yourself?

"If you believed something really big was about to

happen, would you give up on your dream or would you stick with it? Would you lose your cool every time you hit a bad shot or would you immediately focus on the next shot and expect to do something incredible with it? Would you be worried about your future or excited about it? Would you allow yourself to lose hope when life throws another obstacle your way or would you be excited to see what kind of miraculous turnaround was about to come out of it?

"Notice that I'm not telling you to expect *only* great things to come your way. Adversity is inevitable. I'm telling you to expect to overcome it by doing something great with it.

"Some of golf's greatest moments came when players found themselves in the most difficult situations. Some of life's greatest miracles occurred when they seemed most impossible. Only out of the greatest setbacks come the greatest comebacks."

"What if I can't get there?" I said. "What if I can't convince myself a miracle is about to happen or that something really good is going to come out of a bad situation."

"Simple. *Act as if.* Carry yourself as though you believe it. Act as if you believe it and you *will* start to believe it. Try it. You'll see."

Later that night, resting in my bed, my thoughts went to my tender back. I couldn't believe the timing of this injury. Right before the final round of the U.S. Open.

That's when I put Eddie's advice to the test.

*Act as if,* I told myself.

*Act as if something really great is about to happen.*

I began thinking of possibilities instead of problems.

*What if something really big* is *about to happen? What if tomorrow is going to be the greatest moment of my career? What if everything is going to work out better than I ever imagined? What if I'm about to experience some kind of miracle?*

When I started asking myself these types of questions, I didn't notice my back pain at all. I drifted into a peaceful night's sleep, *feeling* like something great was about to happen.

# 44

The U.S. Open's final round always takes place on Father's Day. That morning, Ashley and the kids called in on FaceTime to wish me a Happy Father's Day and good luck in the final round.

"I wish we could be there, but I'm not sure this one is ready for another trip," Ashley said, pointing at our one-year-old with a wink and a smile.

"I think everyone will appreciate the quieter crowd," I said with a laugh.

"You seem in good spirits. How are you feeling? How is your back?"

"Actually, I'm feeling great. It was a little stiff this morning, but I got in some stretching, did a little work on it. It's feeling great now. I've got a really good …" I paused, not wanting to—what, jinx myself?— by expressing too much confidence. Then I decided, go for it. If I believe it, say it.

"I've got a really good feeling about today," I said. "I don't know what it is, but I think something really great is about to happen. I think I might find a way to *win* this thing."

Ashley raised her eyebrows, surprised by what I had

just said. Then a smile came over her. "Wow, Jack, I've never heard you this confident before."

"I've never been this confident before. I just feel like my time has come. I feel very strongly something really big is going to happen today."

# 45

Mike and I were at the driving range to hit some final practice balls before my round began. In sixth place, I would be paired with the fifth-place player and we'd be the third-to-last group to tee off for the final round of the U.S. Open.

In first place was Owen Carmichael III. He and I had a little history. He was a super-talented player known for playing mind games with other players. That's what he would call it: *mind games*. I would call it old-fashioned trash talking.

I beat him in a playoff at the Gateway Championship for my first Tour win three years ago. Since that time, he had joined the LIV Golf tour (another professional tour that competed with the PGA), but LIV players were allowed to compete against PGA players at Major events like this one. Hitting practice balls at the driving range, I was reminded how nice it had been to *not* see Owen much over the past three years.

"Well, if it isn't my old friend, Jackie Boy McKee," he said from behind me, in the middle of my backswing.

I clumsily took a step back, startled by the interruption.

Owen laughed loud with a hand over his stomach, as

though he had just pulled a hilarious prank interrupting my swing. "Sorry, I couldn't resist."

"Owen, you're back," I said.

"Never left, Jackie Boy. I only come in for the Majors now. I've got bigger fish to fry."

I nodded. "Well, good luck to you." I turned my attention back to my teed-up ball, hoping that would end the conversation.

"How's the back feeling?" he said. "Looked pretty painful yesterday. It's always something with you, isn't it?"

I smiled, knowing Owen was trying to get in my head. "Actually, I'm feeling great. Excited to get out there and see what I can do."

"Did I hear you hit the Church Pews *twice* yesterday? Those can be tough; I hope you weren't too hard on yourself. It can happen to the best of us." He paused for a moment before continuing. "But wow, hitting them *twice* in one round? I've never seen *that* before. That is brutal, man."

"It's a tough course," I said with a chuckle, not taking the bait.

"Is Eddie Collins still helping you get your head right? I'd be careful taking too much of his advice. He never did win a U.S. Open, did he?"

I turned back towards Owen, now facing him as I gripped my club tight. "Neither have you, right?"

Owen forced a smile, then looked at his watch. "I plan to have mine in, what, about five hours?"

I shrugged. "Well, good luck to you, Owen."

"I'd say 'thanks,' but I was taught to never believe in luck. You have to make your own."

He strutted towards his assigned hitting bay at the other end of the range.

"Oh, and Owen?" I said.

He turned around. "Yes, Jackie?"

"I'm coming for the win today. Just some friendly advice that you better bring your A-game."

It wasn't like me to engage in talk like this, but I couldn't resist. It caught Owen off-guard. Bullies weren't used to being challenged.

He huffed. "Bold talk for a guy five strokes behind me." He waved me off as he walked away.

"My big brother not backing down," Mike said with a grin.

"He pulls that stuff every time he sees me," I said. "I'm just letting him know I can stand up for myself. And I mean what I said. He better watch out for me."

Mike nodded, liking the confidence he was hearing. "Okay, Jack, let's do this."

I hit my ball and ripped one of the best drives I had hit in months.

"Something really big is about to happen," I said.

# 46

Three holes into the final round of the U.S. Open on a cloudy and soggy afternoon with on-and-off rain at Oakmont, I was feeling good after avoiding the Church Pews on the third hole and parring all three initial holes.

On the fourth hole, I was so worried about the Church Pews to the left that I went too far to the right and landed in a smaller bunker off the fairway.

"At least I missed the Pews," I said to Mike with a laugh as we walked along the fairway.

"Always looking on the bright side," he said, though I could tell he was surprised by my attitude after such a poor shot.

*Something really great is about to happen*, I told myself as we walked.

Eddie was right. As I repeated that message to myself, there was something about the word *about* that made me excited for what might happen next. Even a shot that landed in the bunker was an opportunity to do something great.

Though I did not do anything spectacular on four, I was able to save par.

On the sixth hole, a 196-yard par-3, I missed a great opportunity by landing in the left-side rough on my first shot. I stayed just above the bunker, but I was playing from a very steep hill. I got the ball up and onto the green with my chip shot, but it stopped immediately in the soggy turf, leaving me about ten feet from the cup. My putt for par ended up a few inches short, giving me a bogey and dropping my score to 2 over for the tournament.

The good news is that it seemed like everyone was struggling on this day. Including my old pal, Owen Carmichael III.

At the turn after nine holes, Mike informed me that Owen was having a rougher day than most. He was back at the seventh hole, but had already bogeyed holes one and six. And he had double-bogeyed the third hole. Apparently, he had landed in the Church Pews and had trouble getting out. *It happens to the best of us,* I thought to myself and couldn't help but smile. After seven holes, he had given up 4 strokes and his lead.

I probably shouldn't admit this, but hearing about Owen's struggles gave me some life. I was only 2 over with nine holes to go. The leader—no longer Carmichael—was just 3 strokes in front of me at 1 under.

I began the back nine with a great opportunity on 10, but missed my six-foot birdie putt, which lipped out of the cup. On a course where birdies were so hard to come by, that one stung.

*Something really great is about to happen,* I told myself again.

I parred 11, 12, and 13. Finally, on 14, I ripped one of my better drives of the weekend. My ball came to a stop after going 298 yards. I felt another sharp pain in my back, but it was nothing like the day before. I put the pain out of my mind and reminded myself *everyone* was dealing with something and I was on a mission to do something really great today.

With my approach shot, I landed my ball six feet from the cup. I lined up my putt, took a deep breath, swung my putter, and watched the ball follow the line in my mind perfectly. It rattled into the cup for my first birdie of the day.

Now even for the round and back to 1 over par for the tournament, I parred the next two holes.

The 17th hole was a 314-yard par-4. It was a great opportunity for a guy like me, who could not rely on monster drives. I hit my tee shot 280 yards and straight. It landed right in front of the green, about 35 yards away from the pin. I chipped onto the green and sank a four-foot putt for my second birdie of the day.

I was now 1 under for the day and even for the tournament.

I had caught fire on the final stretch, but was it too late?

# 47

The lead had shifted a few times throughout the final round. First, Owen had played himself out of contention. I'm sure he'd have plenty of excuses, but he was a disastrous 7 over after 16 holes. His playing partner, who had started the day in second place, had the lead for one hole but then struggled near the turn and had fallen behind.

The leader at 1 under was now my playing partner, a good, younger player named Tim Jacobson. He was 1 stroke ahead of me.

As we set up for the 18th and final hole, I could see the nervous tension in his face. In just his second year on the Tour, I knew he was going to be a great player, but the pressure of winning his first Major was going to be a big test for him.

I teed off first thanks to my birdie on 17. I made solid contact, but didn't get much distance as my ball stopped immediately in the damp ground after traveling just 270 yards. However, I was right in the middle of the fairway.

*Something really great is about to happen.*

Jacobson fired his tee shot 30 yards farther than me, but it landed in the wet sand of the left-side bunker.

Two-hundred-and-thirty-yards out from the hole, Mike told me the slope on the green would feed to the right. I flushed my approach shot and thought I had hit it perfectly. My ball initially bounced in front of the green, then carried onto the green. But it was moving faster than I wanted it to. I hoped that the wet grass and the slope to the right would slow my ball down. Unfortunately, I just missed the slope and my ball rolled and rolled and rolled all the way off the back of the green and into the rough behind the green. I was now stuck in the rough 53 feet away from the cup.

I squeezed the grip of my club. I had been too aggressive with my shot. I had blown another golden opportunity.

But then I caught myself.

I took a deep breath.

What if this was the setup for something incredible?

*Act as if a miracle is about to happen*, I reminded myself.

Jacobson flubbed his bunker shot and watched it roll back into the sand. I felt for my colleague. I had certainly been in the same situation before. He was a great young golfer, but the pressure had gotten to him.

His third shot put him on the fairway. His fourth shot landed brilliantly within eight feet of the cup. He would likely bogey the hole, which gave me new life. Though I was in the rough beyond the green, I still had a good shot at making par. If I could do that and if he bogeyed, he and I would be tied for the lead, assuming no one from the group behind us eagled the hole, which had not been done all tournament.

From 53-feet out, I needed to chip in close to the hole. I needed to set myself up for an easy putt for par.

Mike pointed out the various slopes on the green I would need to contend with. This included the ridge on the green I would want to make sure I cleared, the right-to-left slope I would want to catch, and the importance of not being too aggressive and hitting a downward slope just past the hole, which could send my ball far past the cup.

My shot had to be just right to give myself the perfect final putt opportunity.

With my wedge in hand and my ball just an inch or two into the thick, wet rough, I looked toward the flag in the cup on the 18th green. I was elevated above the cup. I wouldn't need to get over an upward ledge or anything like that.

I planted my feet firmly, leaned over my ball and looked to the left at my target again. As I did, I saw a mental line instantly flash in my mind. A line from my ball to the right of the cup and then a curve left directly to the cup. The mental line was there and gone in a split-second, but I saw it. If I handled this chip just right, it was possible—it was at least *possible*—that I could sink this shot and win the tournament.

Was this the *something great* I had been waiting for? Was this the miracle I had been telling myself to expect?

There had been some historic chip-ins throughout golf history. Tom Watson's on the 17th at the 1982 U.S. Open comes instantly to mind. Tiger Wood's chip on the 16th at the 2005 Masters is one of the most-replayed shots in the history of our sport.

But a chip-in from more than 50 feet out to *win* a U.S. Open had never been done. Was it time for such a historic shot? Could *I* be the player who made history?

*Something really great is about to happen.*

What sounded silly and forced the night before was now a phrase I couldn't get out of my head.

*I am about to do something incredible,* I told myself.

I chipped it with my wedge. My ball popped upward and landed on the green about ten feet in front of me. It rolled softly downward, clearing a slight ridge on the green and moving fairly straight ahead. Had I aimed too far to the right for it to catch the slope that would kick it back to the left?

*God, it is in your hands,* I prayed to myself.

Just as it looked like my ball was losing momentum, it started to break to the left, to the left, to the left.

It rolled towards the hole, following the line I had seen in my mind.

But did it have enough speed? Would it come to a stop?

The crowd grew louder and louder as the ball got closer and closer. It crept along slowly on the wet grass, getting closer and closer as it continued to run out of steam.

My ball rolled to within an inch … half an inch … nearly stopping … and then it grabbed the lip of the cup and dropped out of sight and into the hole!

The crowd erupted like I had never heard before at a golf tournament. Mike hugged me from behind, my hat and his flying off. We couldn't believe it!

I had chipped in from more than 50 feet out to win a Major. In the history of golf, it had never been done before.

Something really great—something nearly *miraculous*—had just happened.

History had been made.

# 48

No player in the group behind us came close to eagling the final hole and I won my first Major championship. In the most dramatic way imaginable. Coming back from 5 strokes down. Winning with an odd-defying chip-in on the final hole. It was incredible.

Just four weeks after deciding to hang it up, I was the U.S. Open Champion who would forever be known for one of the most dramatic shots in the history of golf.

Along with the prestige of winning a Major, a Major victory granted players a *five*-year Tour card exemption. My career had some life left in it, after all.

After the trophy ceremony, as I walked to the Oakmont Inn, I couldn't help but think back to when I first returned to a golf course for some practice after my accident. Big swings with my driver were initially out of the question due to my injuries. So, for the first few months of my recovery, all I practiced was putting and chipping. Putting and chipping. Putting and chipping.

It hit me that over the past year, because of my recovery process, I spent more practice time chipping from the edge of the green than I ever had before. I had to wonder if I would have made a shot like the one I made to win the U.S. Open if I had not spent so much extra time practicing my chip shots.

They say God sees the bigger picture and can bring a greater good out of tough situations, often in ways we can't see at the moment. Perhaps me being forced to practice my short game *so* much longer than I ever would have thought practical was one of those times. I suppose only God knows for sure, but I was starting to believe it.

I said a little prayer to myself, thanking God for this moment and telling him I was sorry for not trusting him during the toughest moments of my journey back. It had all worked out better than I could have ever scripted.

What had been one of the worst setbacks I could imagine happening a year before had culminated in the greatest victory of my professional career. It all seemed unreal.

When I got to my room at the Inn, I called Ashley. She couldn't stop crying. I admit to shedding a few tears myself.

I finally knocked on Eddie's door around 9 o'clock that night. I walked in holding the famous U.S. Open trophy – an 18-inch silver cup with handles on both sides and the names of every winner since the first in 1895 etched on the bottom portion. It would be mine to keep for a year.

Debbie gave me a big hug and congratulated me.

"I owe it all to your husband," I said.

Eddie laughed as he pulled me in for a hug. "Please, I don't know who taught you to chip like that, but it sure as hell wasn't me. You know how to make it dramatic."

Soon enough, Mike stopped by and the five of us shared some celebratory drinks on Eddie's balcony.

Around midnight, I was exhausted. It was time to collapse and call it a night.

Before I left, I turned to Eddie with tears in my eyes.

"What you did for me," I said. "You didn't have to do it. You didn't have to care so much. I will never, ever forget it."

I held up my trophy, the one Major trophy he never got.

"This is just as much yours as it is mine," I said.

"It's a funny thing," he said. "Watching you out there, I felt like I was in your shoes. I felt like I was competing again, right along with you. I kept saying, 'something really great is about to happen' all day long. In a strange way, your victory today means more to me than any of the Majors I won. I think it's because I know what you had to overcome. I appreciate you allowing me to be a part of it in whatever small way I could be."

Now Eddie had tears as well. As did Debbie and Mike.

Eddie tapped his temple. "It starts here." Then he tapped his heart. "But it ends up here. What you overcame this year required more heart than anything I've ever seen. You've got something special inside you. Don't ever forget that."

He held out his hand and I shook it tight. He pulled me in for another embrace.

Once again, Eddie Collins had saved my career and changed my life.

# About the Author

**DARRIN DONNELLY** is the bestselling author of *Think Like a Warrior, Relentless Optimism, The Mental Game,* and several other books in the inspirational *Sports for the Soul* series. Though the main characters in Donnelly's books are usually coaches or athletes, they represent anyone with a big dream and the desire to be successful. The seasons and games they endure represent the seasons of life we all must go through when trying to master a new skill, achieve a new goal, or rebound from a setback.

*Sports for the Soul* books help readers fill their minds with motivation and positivity while also learning how to build a winner's mindset, overcome adversity, and achieve their goals—in all areas of life.

Donnelly lives in the suburbs of Kansas City with his wife and three children.

He can be reached at *SportsForTheSoul.com* and on X *@DarrinDonnelly.*

# Sports for the Soul®

This book is part of the *Sports for the Soul* series. For updates on this book, future books, and a free newsletter that delivers advice and inspiration from top coaches, athletes, and sports psychologists, join us at: **SportsForTheSoul.com**.

The *Sports for the Soul* newsletter will help you:

- Find your calling and follow your passion
- Harness the power of positive thinking
- Build your self-confidence
- Attack every day with joy and enthusiasm
- Develop mental toughness
- Increase your energy and stay motivated
- Explore the spiritual side of success
- Be a positive leader for your family and your team
- And much more…

Join us at: **SportsForTheSoul.com**.

## Don't Miss the Start of This Story...

Be sure to read *The Mental Game*, the first bestseller featuring Jack McKee and Eddie Collins. Their story begins when Jack reaches out to Eddie for help with his golf game after a public meltdown on live TV. Eddie teaches Jack that his problem is not in his swing, but in his mind. *The Mental Game* is about much more than golf. It's about winning the mental battle we all must face on a daily basis.

Grab your copy of *The Mental Game* wherever books are sold.

## Check out the previous books in the *Sports for the Soul* series...

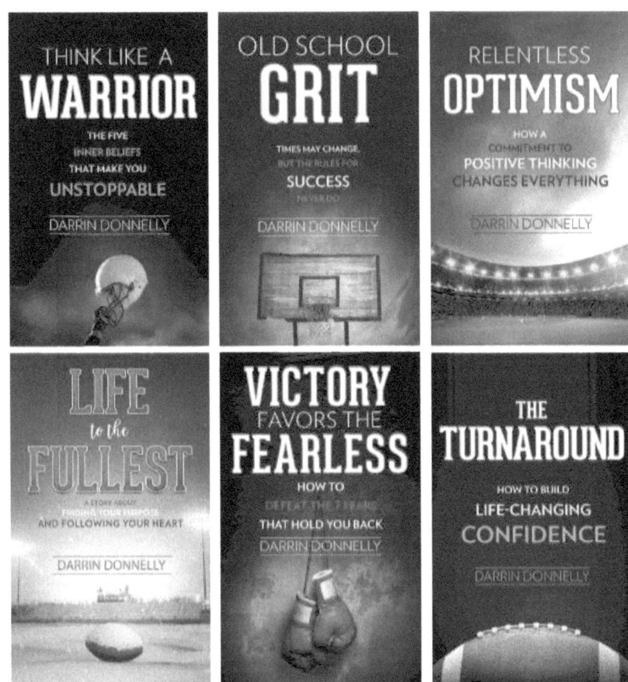

For more information, visit **SportsForTheSoul.com**

www.ingramcontent.com/pod-product-compliance
Lightning Source LLC
LaVergne TN
LVHW100528110826
845146LV00002B/814

*9798988010227*